JOSEPH HAYDN

SYMPHONY No. 104

D major/D-Dur/Ré majeur
Hob. I:104
'London'

Edited by
Harry Newstone

Ernst Eulenburg Ltd

London · Mainz · Madrid · New York · Paris · Prague · Tokyo · Toronto · Zürich

CONTENTS

Ernst Eulenburg Ltd
48 Great Marlborough Street
London W1F 7BB

PREFACE

In the autumn of 1790 Prince Nikolaus Joseph Esterházy, Haydn's employer and patron, died and his son, Prince Paul Anton, succeeded him. Almost at once the great (but considerably expensive) musical establishment which had for nearly 30 years nurtured the composer, and is now chiefly remembered for the glory he brought to it, was dismantled. Although still nominally Kapellmeister, with a yearly pension, Haydn was at last free to travel wherever he wished, something he had not been able to do before. He returned to Vienna relieved of the daily pressures of court duties, but his respite was not to last long. Johann Peter Salomon, the German-born violinist and London impresario, was visiting Cologne when he heard of the death of Prince Nikolaus and lost no time in getting to Vienna determined to procure Haydn for his forthcoming London season. It was not the first time he had invited Haydn to England; now the composer was free to accept, and he did. A contract was exchanged and the two left Vienna in the middle of December and arrived in Dover on New Year's Day 1791.

Haydn stayed in England for a year and a half and returned for a second visit of similar duration in 1794–5. The stimulus he received from the London musical scene, the reception he was accorded there and the high quality of the musicians placed at his disposal inspired him to some of his finest music. The 12 symphonies he wrote for Salomon (six for each visit) are the summation of his orchestral achievement and the ground upon which the music he composed after his return to Vienna – notably the last six masses, *The Creation* and *The Seasons* – was based.

The most popular of the London symphonies are among the most frequently played of Haydn's works, yet for very many years they were (and often still are) performed from texts that had, during the 19th century, become seriously corrupted from the originals. The first modern attempt to present a uniform set of scores based upon authentic sources came with Ernst Praetorius's edition for Eulenburg in the 1930s. For this he consulted the autograph scores of Nos. 98, 99, 101, 102, 103 and 104 but not those of Nos. 94, 95, 96 and 100 (No. 93 has disappeared and the whereabouts of No. 97 was then unknown). One can only speculate on why Praetorius was not able to examine the autograph of No. 94 which was in the then Preußische Staatsbibliothek in Berlin, where he had seen those of Nos. 98, 99, 101, 102 and 104, or Nos. 95 and 96 which were in the British Museum along with No. 103 of which he had received a photocopy. Clearly, detailed knowledge of the whereabouts of Haydn autographs was still very sketchy in the 1930s and Praetorius probably had no way of knowing what we, with the benefit of a further 50 years of Haydn research, can take for granted. Thus Praetorius's edition, while the best available at the time and certainly an important step in the right direction was, not surprisingly, uneven.

The phase of Haydn research that was to result in no less than a renaissance was now well begun. In 1939 the distinguished Danish scholar Jens Peter Larsen published *Die Haydn-Überlieferung* and two years later a facsimile print of *Drei Haydn-Kataloge*, revealing for the first time the immensity of the subject. The postwar years saw the formation in London of the Haydn Orchestra and in Boston of the Haydn Society (both 1949). In 1954, the founder of the Haydn Society, H. C. Robbins Landon, in an article 'The original versions of Haydn's first 'Salomon' symphonies',[1] drew our attention to the extent to which the standard performing editions of these works (mostly Breitkopf & Härtel and Peters) were in many cases 'flagrant falsifications of Haydn's own texts'. For a discussion on how these alterations came about

[1] *The Music Review*, Vol. 15/1, 1954

the reader is referred to that article as well as to Landon's *The Symphonies of Joseph Haydn*,[2] and his *Haydn – Chronicle and Works*, Vol. 3 *Haydn in England*.[3]

Since the mid-1950s Henle Verlag, Munich, has issued a number of volumes of Haydn symphonies as part of a Complete Edition of his works for the Haydn Institute of Cologne. Universal Edition, Vienna, issued all the symphonies during the 1960s in an edition by H. C. Robbins Landon.

In 1959, the present writer, with material and advice from Professor Landon, revised and conducted all the London symphonies in a series of BBC broadcasts commemorating the 150th anniversary of the composer's death. The aim was to get as close as possible to Haydn's original intentions not only from the scholar's point of view but from the performer's too.

The texts were accordingly prepared from a number of manuscript sources of primary authenticity and one early printed edition of unusual interest and importance. These same sources, which are listed below with their credentials, have been re-examined for this new edition together with other more recent discoveries.

Editorial Notes

Location and description of sources

I. Autograph scores and authentic manuscript copies

We retain, for convenience, the generally accepted numerical order established by Eusebius von Mandyczewski for the Breitkopf & Härtel Collected Edition (begun in 1907 but never completed) although, in the case of the first set of London symphonies, this is not thought to be the order in which they were composed or first performed.

No. 93 Autograph:
Whereabouts unknown, possibly lost. Seen in a Brunswick bookshop in 1870 by the Haydn biographer, Carl Ferdinand Pohl, who noted the date 1791 on it in Haydn's hand.
Copies:
1. Copy made in London for Salomon, with corrections in other hands – possibly Haydn's and Salomon's. Acquired by the Royal Philharmonic Society in 1847 from William Ayrton who had inherited all of Salomon's music in 1815. Acquired by the British Library, London, January 1988.[4]
2. Copy made by Esterházy copyist (Elßler or another with similar handwriting). Esterházy Archives, National Széchényi Library, Budapest.

No. 94 Autograph:
Movements I, III and IV in the Staatsbibliothek zu Berlin – Preußischer Kulturbesitz, Musikabteilung, lacking last page of Mov. I and the first two pages of the Minuet. The missing page of Mov. I and the whole of Mov. II (in its original version before Haydn added the 'surprise') in the Library of Congress, Washington, D.C.
Copies:
1. Salomon's London copy; details as No. 93.
2. Esterházy copy; details as No. 93.
Both with later version of Mov. II (i.e., with 'surprise').

No. 95 Autograph:
Royal Philharmonic Society collection, British Library, London. Bound together with autograph of No. 96 and copy of No. 98.
Copies:
None found – see III below.

No. 96 Autograph:
Royal Philharmonic Society collection, British Library, London. Bound together with autograph of No. 95 and copy of No. 98.
Copies:

[2] London, 1955
[3] London, 1976

[4] see Arthur Searle, 'Haydn Manuscripts in the British Library', *Early Music*, 5/1982, also *Haydn Yearbook* XIV

None found – see III below.

No. 97 Autograph:
Owned by Mrs Eva Alberman, London (formerly Stefan Zweig collection); acquired by the British Library, London, May 1986.
Copy:
Salomon's London copy; details as No. 93.

No. 98 Autograph:
Formerly in the Preußische Staatsbibliothek, Berlin (from the Schindler Beethoven collection). Four pages missing from Mov. IV. Now in the Jagellonian University Library, Krakow.
Copy:
Salomon's London copy; details as No. 93. Bound together with the autographs of Nos. 95 and 96.

No. 99 Autograph:
Formerly in the Preußische Staatsbibliothek, Berlin. Now in the Jagellonian University Library, Krakow. Photocopy in Hoboken Photogramm Archiv, Vienna.
Copies:
1. Salomon's London copy; details as No. 93.
2. Elßler copy, Esterházy Archives, National Széchényi Library, Budapest.

No. 100 Autograph:
Esterházy Archives, National Széchényi Library, Budapest, lacking Mov. II.
Copy:
Salomon's London copy; details as No. 93.

No. 101 Autograph:
Formerly in the Preußische Staatsbibliothek, Berlin. Now in the Jagellonian University Library, Krakow. Photocopy in Hoboken Photogramm Archiv, Vienna.
Copies:
1. Salomon's London copy; details as No. 93.
2. Elßler copy, Esterházy Archives, National Széchényi Library, Budapest.

No. 102 Autograph:
Staatsbibliothek zu Berlin – Preußischer Kulturbesitz, Musikabteilung, Berlin.
Copy:
Salomon's London copy; details as No. 93.

No. 103 Autograph:
British Library, London: three pages of Minuet in another hand.
Copy:
Salomon's London copy; details as No. 93.

No. 104 Autograph:
Staatsbibliothek zu Berlin – Preußischer Kulturbesitz, Musikabteilung, Berlin.
Copy:
Salomon's London copy; details as No. 93.

It will be seen that, with the exception of No. 93 and the missing slow movement of No. 100, the autograph scores of the London symphonies have survived very nearly intact. The copies made for Salomon in London are a recent (1982) discovery by Alec Hyatt King, and are of great importance.

II. Manuscript orchestral material by Johann Elßler

Orchestral parts copied from the autograph scores by Haydn's own copyist, many with corrections in the composer's hand, are obviously of great value in the establishment of accurate texts of the London symphonies. The most comprehensive collection of the London symphonies is in the Fürstenberg Archives, Donaueschingen, which has them all but No. 100. Some of these parts are on English paper and were evidently used in the original London performances before being taken back to Vienna by Haydn. The Esterházy Archives in Budapest have Elßler parts of Nos. 95, 96, 97, 99, 100, 101 and 103 (the latter lacking the Minuet), and the Oettingen-Wallerstein Archives in Harburg have Nos. 93, 96, 97 and 98.

III. London manuscript scores

In 1795 and 1796 respectively, Haydn presented Salomon with the exclusive rights to both sets of London symphonies, a very proper gesture to the man who had commissioned them and had led the orchestra for the first performances of nine of them (the last three symphonies were presented by the newly-formed 'Opera Concert' at the King's Theatre under the direction of Giovanni Battista Viotti). The tangible aspect of this handsome gift was a complete set of scores – the autographs of Nos. 95 and 96 and copies of the rest, as set out in I above. In November 1791, Haydn sent copy scores of Nos. 95 and 96 to his friend in Vienna, Bernhard von Kees. They evidently arrived safely since von Kees entered the opening bars of both works in his catalogue of Haydn symphonies with the words 'NB von London gekommen', but these scores have not been located.

IV. Printed orchestral material by Robert Birchall, London

There can be no doubt that Salomon also had his own personal set of orchestral parts of all 12 symphonies. He had them engraved, after Haydn's return to Vienna (as the terms of the presentation entitled him to do), with at least one publisher (Monzani & Cimador) and he may also have sold them to others. A year or two after Haydn's death (1809) Salomon entered into an agreement with Robert Birchall (who had earlier published Salomon's arrangements for Piano Trio and for Flute and String Quartet with optional Piano of the London symphonies) for a new issue of the orchestral parts. If Landon is right in supposing that Salomon provided Birchall with his own performing material for this print – possibly the very material he had used under Haydn's direction – it would explain not only the high intelligence and practical nature of the editings, but, more important, the often close relationship between Birchall and the autographs, and the even closer relationship between Birchall and the copy scores that Haydn presented to Salomon.

The Birchall print thus has a high place among the sources upon which this edition is based. With so strong a link – Salomon – between it and Haydn and its readiness as a performing edition, it has a combination of virtues that will be of interest to both scholars and performers. Where the Birchall differs from our other sources (generally because of changes that Haydn made after his return to Vienna that would have been unknown to Salomon) such variants, as well as others of interest, are shown in the Textual Notes below.

Editorial method

Redundant cautionary or parallel accidentals have in some cases been omitted. Haydn's habit of reminding players constantly of such accidentals in continuously modulating passages, even if it means repeating them in the same bar, makes it difficult to follow this aim with complete consistency, and in such cases we have omitted only those which, in modern practice, might confuse rather than clarify.

Missing accidentals, staccato signs, slurs, ties and dynamics etc., have been added without comment only where their absence is the obvious result of the composer's, copyist's or engraver's oversight. Where explanatory comment may be helpful this will be found in the Textual Notes below.

Square brackets and broken ties and slurs indicate editorial additions in the text. The basis for such additions (i.e. parallel or analogous passages) will be clear by the context.

We have retained the indication *Tutti* (used by Haydn to cancel a previous *Solo*, usually in the woodwind) wherever it appears in our sources. Where it is clearly implied by the context but not shown in any of the sources, we have used the modern equivalent – [a 2] where the two parts are in unison.

Since Haydn and Elßler generally wrote a staccato as a quick stroke, it is difficult to determine whether a difference in performance is intended between a stroke and a dot. In general we have used dots except where a sharply accented staccato seems required.

SYMPHONY No. 104

Haydn's last symphony – 'The 12th which I have composed in England', as he wrote on the cover of the autograph score – was first performed in the New Room, King's Theatre, Haymarket, London on 4 May 1795. Haydn would have 'presided' at the keyboard and the 'Leader of the Band' was probably William (Wilhelm) Cramer, at whose benefit concert Haydn had taken part only three days earlier. Although Haydn had moved over to G.B. Viotti's Opera Concert series upon the discontinuance earlier that year of Salomon's concerts (for which the two sets of six 'London' symphonies had been commissioned), the occasion on 4 May was not one of Viotti's subscription series but a special event – 'Dr Haydn's Night' – in benefit of the composer.

The new symphony was rapturously received and was no doubt repeated at one of the remaining subscription concerts (held 11 and 18 May) or at one of the additional concerts in which Haydn participated before leaving for Vienna on 15 August. In his notebook he wrote of the 4 May concert:

> The whole company was thoroughly pleased, and so was I. I made four thousand gulden on this evening. Such a thing is only possible in England.[5]

On 18 December 1795, Haydn organised a concert in the small Redoutensaal in Vienna at which, to quote from the *Wiener Zeitung*, 'three grand symphonies, not yet heard here, which Herr Kapellmeister composed during his last sojourn in London, will be performed'.[6] The 'Military' Symphony was one of these[7] and Ernst Praetorius, in his 1936 Eulenberg edition of the symphony, claims that No. 104 was first heard in Vienna on this occasion (at which, it might also be noted, Beethoven played his Second Piano Concerto).

The main theme of the finale is said to be based on the Croatian folk-song 'Oj Jelena', whose first 12 bars are quoted below but after which the resemblance ends. It has also been suggested that it originated in a London street cry, 'Hot Cross Buns'[8] or another 'Live Cod' but there is no evidence to support this and its closeness to the Croatian tune can leave little doubt as to its provenance.

For some reason the title 'London' or 'Salomon', which should apply to all 12 of Haydn's last symphonies, seems to have been attached to this particular work.

Sources

Autograph score in the Music Collection of the Staatsbibliothek zu Berlin – Preußischer Kulturbesitz, Berlin . . . . AUT

Copy of the score made by a London copyist, in the British Library, London . . . . LON

Manuscript material in what looks like Johann Elßler's hand (except for Vl. I/II), in the Fürstenberg Archives, Donaueschingen . . . . . D/E

Printed parts by Birchall . . . . BIR

Birchall's edition of Salomon's Quintet arrangement SAL5

Harry Newstone

[5] H.C.Robbins Landon, *Haydn – Chronicle and Works* (Vol. 3 *Haydn in England*), (London, 1976), 309
[6] H.C.Robbins Landon, *Haydn – Chronicle and Works* (Vol. 4 *The Years of the Creation*), (London, 1977), 59
[7] ibid., 60
[8] op. cit., Vol. III, 614–15

VORWORT

Im Herbst 1790 starb Fürst Nikolaus Joseph Esterházy, Haydns Dienstherr und Gönner; Fürst Paul Anton, sein Sohn, folgte ihm nach. Fast unmittelbar hierauf wurde das bedeutende, allerdings ziemlich kostspielige Musikleben am Hofe eingestellt, das Haydn nahezu dreißig Jahre lang ernährt hatte, und an das man sich heute hauptsächlich des Glanzes wegen erinnert, den es durch den Komponisten erhalten hatte. Obwohl er auch weiterhin den Kapellmeistertitel führen durfte und eine jährliche Pension erhielt, konnte Haydn im Gegensatz zu früher nun schließlich nach Belieben reisen. Er kehrte nach Wien zurück, entlastet vom täglichen Zwang des Dienstes am Hofe, jedoch sollte diese Ruhepause nicht von langer Dauer sein. Als der deutschstämmige Geiger und Londoner Impresario Johann Peter Salomon während eines Aufenthaltes in Köln vom Tod des Fürsten Nikolaus erfuhr, eilte er unverzüglich nach Wien, entschlossen, Haydn für die kommende Saison nach London zu verpflichten. Dies war nicht das erste Mal, dass er Haydn nach England eingeladen hatte; jetzt jedoch war der Komponist in der Lage zuzusagen, und er tat es auch. Ein Vertrag wurde ausgehandelt, und die beiden verließen Wien Mitte Dezember und erreichten Dover am Neujahrstag 1791.

Haydn blieb anderthalb Jahre lang in England und kehrte 1794/95 zu einem zweiten, etwa gleich langen Aufenthalt zurück. Die Anregungen, die er durch das Londoner Musikleben erhielt, die Aufnahme dort und die hohe Qualität der ihm zur Verfügung stehenden Musiker inspirierten ihn zu mehreren seiner bedeutendsten Werke. So bilden die zwölf Sinfonien für Salomon (sechs für jeden Aufenthalt) die Zusammenfassung seiner ganzen Kunst der Orchesterkomposition und die Grundlage für die Werke, die er nach seiner Rückkehr nach Wien schrieb – vor allem die sechs letzten Messen sowie die *Schöpfung* und die *Jahreszeiten*.

Die bekanntesten der Londoner Sinfonien gehören zu den meistgespielten Werken Haydns, jedoch wurden sie viele Jahre lang (vielfach noch bis in die heutige Zeit) aus Notenmaterial aufgeführt, das im 19. Jahrhundert gegenüber dem Originaltext erheblich verfälscht worden war. Den ersten neueren Versuch, aufgrund der authentischen Quellen einen einheitlichen Satz Partituren herauszubringen, stellt die Ausgabe von Ernst Praetorius im Rahmen der Edition Eulenburg in den 1930er Jahren dar. Er zog die Partitur-Autographe von Nr. 98, 99, 101, 102, 103 und 104 heran, nicht aber diejenigen von Nr. 94, 95, 96 und 100 (das Autograph von Nr. 93 ist verschollen, und das von Nr. 97 war damals nicht nachweisbar). Man kann nur Vermutungen darüber anstellen, warum Praetorius nicht in der Lage war, das Autograph von Nr. 94 zu untersuchen, das in der damaligen Preußischen Staatsbibliothek in Berlin lag, wo er auch die Autographe von Nr. 98, 99, 101, 102 und 104 eingesehen hatte; Nr. 95 und 96 waren ihm im British Museum London zugänglich, zusammen mit dem Autograph von Nr. 103, das ihm als Fotokopie vorlag. Auf jeden Fall war die Kenntnis der Aufbewahrungsorte von Haydn-Autographen in den 1930er Jahren noch sehr lückenhaft, und Praetorius konnte damals wohl kaum wissen, was wir heute, nach weiteren 50 Jahren Haydn-Forschung, als erwiesen betrachten können. So war es nicht verwunderlich, dass die Ausgaben von Praetorius in sich uneinheitlich waren, auch wenn sie zu ihrer Zeit die besten verfügbaren waren und sicherlich einen Schritt in die richtige Richtung unternahmen.

Damit hatte eine Zeit intensiver Haydn-Forschung begonnen, die eine regelrechte Renaissance auslöste. 1939 veröffentlichte der bedeutende dänische Musikwissenschaftler Jens Peter Larsen sein Buch *Die Haydn-Überlieferung* und zwei Jahre später als Faksimile *Drei Haydn-Kataloge*; damit wies er erstmals auf die nahezu unüberschaubaren Dimensionen dieses Forschungsbereichs hin. In den Nachkriegsjahren folgten die Gründung des Haydn-Orchesters London und in Boston die der Haydn-Gesellschaft (beide 1949). 1954 machte H. C. Robbins Landon, Begründer der Haydn-Gesellschaft, in einem Aufsatz „The original versions of Haydn's first 'Salomon' symphonies"[1] auf das Ausmaß aufmerksam, in dem das verfügbare Aufführungsmaterial dieser Werke (hauptsächlich von Breitkopf & Härtel und Peters) in vielen Fällen durch „offenkundige Verfälschung von Haydns eigenem Notentext" entstellt war. Bezüglich einer eingehenden Darstellung, wie es zu diesen Abweichungen kam, sei hier auf den zitierten Aufsatz sowie auf Landons Arbeiten *The Symphonies of Joseph Haydn*[2] und *Haydn – Chronicle and Works* (Bd. 3: *Haydn in England*)[3] hingewiesen.

Seit Mitte der 1950er Jahre hat der Henle-Verlag München im Rahmen einer Gesamtausgabe der Werke Haydns durch das Haydn-Institut Köln mehrere Bände mit Sinfonien veröffentlicht. Bei der Universal Edition Wien erschienen alle Sinfonien in den 1960er Jahren in einer Ausgabe von H. C. Robbins Landon.

1959 revidierte der Herausgeber der hier vorliegenden Ausgabe anlässlich einer Sendereihe der BBC zum 150. Todestage des Komponisten, in der er selbst alle Londoner Sinfonien Haydns dirigierte, die Partituren, wofür ihm Robbins Landon eigenes Material und seinen Rat zur Verfügung stellte. Das Ziel war, Haydns eigenen Intentionen nicht nur vom wissenschaftlichen Standpunkt aus, sondern auch aus der Sicht des ausübenden Musikers so nahe wie möglich zu kommen.

Der Notentext wurde aufgrund einer Anzahl handschriftlicher Primärquellen und einer besonders interessanten und wichtigen Druckausgabe erarbeitet. Diese unten verzeichneten und beschriebenen Quellen wurden für die Neuausgabe unter Berücksichtigung anderer neuerer Forschungsergebnisse nochmals untersucht.

[1] *The Music Review*, Jg. 15/1, 1954.
[2] London 1955.
[3] London 1976.

Revisionsbericht

Quellen-Fundorte und Quellenbeschreibung

I. Partiturautographe und autorisierte Abschriften

Der Einfachheit halber wird die allgemein übliche Zählung nach der Gesamtausgabe von Eusebius von Mandyczewski bei Breitkopf & Härtel (unvollständig, begonnen 1907) beibehalten, obwohl sie vermutlich für die erste Folge der Londoner Sinfonien weder der Reihenfolge der Entstehung noch der Uraufführungen entspricht.

Nr. 93 Autograph:
Verschollen, möglicherweise verloren. Zuletzt 1870 in einer Braunschweiger Buchhandlung durch den Haydn-Biographen Carl Ferdinand Pohl nachgewiesen, der die Datierung 1791 von Haydns Hand feststellte.
Abschriften:
1. Abschrift aus London, angefertigt für Salomon, mit Korrekturen in anderer Handschrift – vermutlich von Haydn und Salomon. 1847 erworben durch die Royal Philharmonic Society London von William Ayrton, der 1815 von Salomon dessen gesamten Bestand an Noten geerbt hatte. Seit Januar 1988 im Besitz der British Library London[4].
2. Abschrift eines Kopisten am Hofe Esterházy (Elßler, der Haydns Kopist war, oder jemand mit ähnlicher Handschrift): Esterházy-Archiv der Széchényi-National-bibliothek Budapest.

Nr. 94 Autograph:
Satz I, III und IV: Staatsbibliothek zu Berlin – Preußischer Kulturbesitz, Musikabteilung (ohne die letzte Seite von Satz I und die ersten beiden Seiten des Menuetts). Die fehlende Seite von Satz I und der vollständige Satz II (in seiner ursprünglichen Fassung vor der

[4] Vgl. Arthur Searle, „Haydn Manuscripts in the British Library", in: *Early Music*, 5/1982, und *Haydn Jahrbuch XIV*.

Hinzufügung des „Paukenschlags" durch Haydn) befinden sich in der Library of Congress Washington D.C.
Abschriften:
1. Salomons Londoner Abschrift; wie Nr. 93
2. Abschrift Esterházy: wie Nr. 93 (beide mit der späteren Fassung von Satz II, d.h. mit dem „Paukenschlag")

Nr. 95 Autograph:
Royal Philharmonic Society Sammlung, British Library London (zusammengebunden mit dem Autograph von Nr. 96 und der Abschrift von Nr. 98)
Abschriften:
Nicht nachweisbar (vgl. unten Abschnitt III)

Nr. 96 Autograph:
Royal Philharmonic Society Sammlung, British Library London (zusammengebunden mit dem Autograph von Nr. 95 und der Abschrift von Nr. 98)
Abschriften:
Nicht nachweisbar (vgl. unten Abschnitt III)

Nr. 97 Autograph:
Im Mai 1986 aus dem Besitz von Frau Eva Alberman, London, erworben durch die British Library London (vormals Sammlung Stefan Zweig).
Abschrift:
Salomons Londoner Abschrift; wie Nr. 93

Nr. 98 Autograph:
Vormals Preußische Staatsbibliothek Berlin (aus der Beethoven-Sammlung Schindlers). Von Satz IV fehlen vier Seiten. Heute im Besitz der Biblioteka Jagielloæska Krakau.
Abschrift:
Salomons Londoner Abschrift; wie Nr. 93 (zusammengebunden mit den Autographen von Nr. 95 und 96)

Nr. 99 Autograph:
Vormals Preußische Staatsbibliothek Berlin; heute im Besitz der Biblioteka Jagielloæska Krakau. Fotokopien im Photogramm-Archiv Hoboken, Wien
Abschriften:
1. Salomons Londoner Abschrift; wie Nr. 93
2. Abschrift Elßler: Esterházy-Archiv der Széchényi-Nationalbibliothek Budapest

Nr. 100 Autograph:
Esterházy-Archiv der Széchényi-Nationalbibliothek Budapest (ohne Satz II)
Abschrift:
Salomons Londoner Abschrift; wie Nr. 93

Nr. 101 Autograph:
Vormals Preußische Staatsbibliothek Berlin; heute im Besitz der Biblioteka Jagielloæska, Krakau. Fotokopien im Photogramm-Archiv Hoboken, Wien
Abschriften:
1. Salomons Londoner Abschrift; wie Nr. 93
2. Abschrift Elßler: Esterházy-Archiv der Széchényi-Nationalbibliothek Budapest

Nr. 102 Autograph:
Staatsbibliothek zu Berlin – Preußischer Kulturbesitz, Musikabteilung
Abschrift:
Salomons Londoner Abschrift; wie Nr. 93

Nr. 103 Autograph:
British Library London (drei Seiten des Menuetts in fremder Handschrift)
Abschrift:
Salomons Londoner Abschrift; wie Nr. 93

Nr. 104 Autograph:
Staatsbibliothek zu Berlin –Preußischer Kulturbesitz, Musikabteilung
Abschrift:
Salomons Londoner Abschrift; wie Nr. 93

Mit Ausnahme von Nr. 93 und dem fehlenden langsamen Satz von Nr. 100 sind also die autographen Partituren der Londoner Sinfonien nahezu unversehrt erhalten. Die Abschriften, die in London für Salomon angefertigt worden waren, wurden erst kürzlich (1982) von Alec Hyatt King entdeckt; sie sind außerordentlich wichtig.

II. Handschriftliches Orchestermaterial von Johann Elßler

Orchesterstimmen, die nach den autographen Partituren von Haydns eigenem Kopisten geschrieben wurden, viele mit Korrekturen in der Handschrift des Komponisten, sind selbstverständlich von großem Wert bei der Ermittlung eines zuverlässigen Notentextes für die Londoner Sinfonien. Die umfassendste Sammlung ist im Besitz des Fürstenbergischen Archivs in Donaueschingen, wo alle Londoner Sinfonien außer Nr. 100 vorhanden sind. Einige dieser Stimmen sind auf Papier englischer Herkunft geschrieben und offenbar bei den Londoner Aufführungen benutzt worden, bevor Haydn sie mit zurück nach Wien nahm. Das Esterházy-Archiv in Budapest besitzt Stimmen von Elßler zu Nr. 95, 96, 97, 99, 100, 101 und 103 (diese ohne Menuett), und das Archiv Oettingen-Wallerstein in Harburg Nr. 93, 96, 97 und 98.

III. Londoner handschriftliche Partituren

1795 bzw. 1796 übertrug Haydn die Exklusivrechte beider Folgen der Londoner Sinfonien an Salomon – eine noble Geste dem Mann gegenüber, der sie in Auftrag gegeben hatte und unter dessen Leitung als Konzertmeister neun von ihnen uraufgeführt worden waren (die letzten drei Sinfonien wurden im King's Theatre vom neu gegründeten „Opera Concert" unter der Leitung von Giovanni Battista Viotti aufgeführt.) Der „materielle Aspekt" dieses noblen Geschenks bestand aus einem vollständigen Satz Partituren – den Autographen von Nr. 95 und 96 und Kopien der restlichen Werke, wie in Abschnitt I ausgeführt. Im November 1791 schickte Haydn Abschriften der Partituren von Nr. 95 und 96 an seinen Wiener Freund Bernhard von Kees. Offenbar sind sie wohlbehalten angekommen, denn von Kees setzte zu den Anfangstakten beider Werke in seinem Verzeichnis der Sinfonien Haydns den Vermerk hinzu: „NB von London gekommen". Die Partituren selbst wurden allerdings bisher nicht aufgefunden.

IV. Gedrucktes Orchestermaterial von Robert Birchall, London

Zweifellos besaß auch Salomon von allen zwölf Sinfonien seinen eigenen Satz Orchesterstimmen. Nach Haydns Rückkehr nach Wien ließ er sie (wozu er nach den Bedingungen der Übereignung berechtigt war) von wenigstens einem Verleger stechen (Monzani & Cimador), und möglicherweise hat er sie außerdem an weitere verkauft. Ein oder zwei Jahre nach Haydns Tod (1809) schloss Salomon eine Vereinbarung mit Robert Birchall (der schon zuvor Salomons Bearbeitungen der Londoner Sinfonien für Klaviertrio sowie für Flöte und Streichquartett und Klavier ad libitum veröffentlicht hatte) über eine Neuausgabe der Orchesterstimmen. Falls Landon mit seiner Annahme recht hat, dass Salomon für diesen Druck Birchall sein eigenes Orchestermaterial zur Verfügung stellte – möglicherweise dasselbe Material, das er bereits unter Haydns Leitung benutzt hatte –, würde dies nicht nur den hohen Standard und den praktischen Charakter der Ausgaben erklären, sondern darüber hinaus auch die oft enge Beziehung zwischen den Stimmen von Birchall und den Autographen und – mit sogar noch größerer Übereinstimmung – zwischen dem Birchall-Druck und den Partitur-Abschriften, die Haydn Salomon geschenkt hatte.

Der Birchall-Druck besitzt also unter den Quellen, auf denen die vorliegende Edition basiert, einen hohen Stellenwert. Mit seiner so engen Beziehung – in der Person Salomons – zu Haydn selbst und mit seiner Tauglichkeit als Aufführungsmaterial verbindet er Vorzüge miteinander, die sowohl für Wissenschaftler wie auch ausübende Musiker von Interesse sind. Wo Birchall von unseren übrigen Quellen abweicht (die Ursache besteht hauptsächlich in Änderungen, die Haydn nach seiner Rückkehr nach Wien vornahm und die Salomon deshalb unbekannt bleiben mussten), werden die Varianten neben anderen wesentlichen

Lesarten in den Einzelanmerkungen unten ausgewiesen.

Editionsprinzipien

Überflüssige Vorsichts- oder wiederholte Akzidentien wurden in einigen Fällen gestrichen. Haydns Gewohnheit, in kontinuierlich modulierenden Passagen den Spielern solche Akzidentien zur Erinnerung fortwährend vorzuschreiben, selbst wenn sie dadurch im selben Takt wiederholt werden, erschwert es, dieses Prinzip konsequent durchzuhalten. In solchen Fällen wurden nur diejenigen Zeichen getilgt, die nach heutigem Gebrauch den Spieler eher verwirren, als dass sie Klarheit schaffen.

Fehlende Akzidentien, Staccato-Zeichen, Artikulations- und Bindebögen, dynamische Bezeichnungen etc. wurden stillschweigend nur dann ergänzt, wenn sie offensichtlich vom Komponisten, Kopisten oder Stecher übersehen wurden. Wenn eine Erläuterung angebracht erscheint, ist sie unten in den Einzelanmerkungen zu finden.

Mit eckigen Klammern und als gestrichelte Bögen sind Herausgeberzusätze im Notentext gekennzeichnet. Die Begründung für solche Ergänzungen (parallele oder analoge Lesarten) ergibt sich aus dem Kontext.

Die Bezeichnung *Tutti*, die Haydn gewöhnlich in den Holzbläserstimmen verwendete, um ein vorausgegangenes Solo aufzuheben, wurde beibehalten, wo es in den benutzten Quellen erscheint. An Stellen, an denen eine Bezeichnung nach dem Kontext eindeutig erforderlich, in den Quellen jedoch nicht ersichtlich ist, wurde das heute übliche [a2] gesetzt, wenn zwei Stimmen unisono spielen.

Da Haydn und Elßler die Staccato-Vorschrift in aller Regel als flüchtig dahingeworfenen Strich notierten, ist die Entscheidung schwierig, ob Strich und Punkt unterschiedlich ausgeführt werden sollen. Der Herausgeber hat grundsätzlich Punkte gesetzt, es sei denn, ein scharf akzentuiertes staccato schien gefordert.

SINFONIE Nr. 104

Haydns letzte Sinfonie – „The 12th which I have composed in England“ wie er selbst in Englisch auf dem Titelblatt der autographen Partitur vermerkte – wurde am 4. Mai 1795 im New Room des King's Theatre am Londoner Haymarket uraufgeführt. Haydn leitete wohl vom Cembalo aus, Konzertmeister war vermutlich William (Wilhelm) Cramer, an dessen Benefizkonzert Haydn gerade drei Tage zuvor teilgenommen hatte. Nachdem Salomon Anfang des Jahres 1795 seine eigenen Konzerte (für welche die beiden Folgen der jeweils sechs Londoner Sinfonien in Auftrag gegeben worden waren) aufgegeben hatte, schloss Haydn sich zwar G. B. Viottis Opera Concerts an, aber die Aufführung am 4. Mai fand nicht im Rahmen der Abonnementskonzerte Viottis statt, sondern war ein Sonderkonzert – „Dr. Haydn's Night“ – zu Gunsten des Komponisten.

Die neue Sinfonie wurde vom Publikum begeistert aufgenommen und zweifellos in einem der weiteren Abonnementskonzerte am 11. und am 18. Mai wiederholt, oder aber in einem der Zusatzkonzerte, an denen Haydn vor seiner Rückkehr nach Wien am 15. August noch teilnahm. Über das Konzert am 4. Mai schrieb er in sein Notizbuch:

> Die ganze Gesellschaft war äußerst vergnügt und auch ich. Ich machte diesen Abend vier tausend Gulden. So etwas kann man nur in England machen.[5]

Am 18. Dezember veranstaltete Haydn im Kleinen Redoutensaal in Wien ein Konzert, bei dem laut *Wiener Zeitung*[6] „drei, hier noch nicht gehörte, große Symphonien, welche der Herr Kapellmeister während seines letzten Aufenthaltes in London verfertigt hat, aufgeführt werden sollen“. Die „Militär“-Sinfonie (Nr. 100) war

[5] Zitiert nach Georg August Griesinger, *Biographische Notizen über Joseph Haydn*, Leipzig 1820, Reprint Leipzig 1979, S. 53.

[6] Vom 6. Dezember; zitiert nach Alexander Wheelock Thayer, *Ludwig van Beethovens Leben*. Nach dem Original-Manuskript deutsch bearbeitet und ergänzt von Hermann Deiters, I. Bd. Leipzig ²1901, S. 387.

[7] Ebda.

eine davon[7], und Ernst Praetorius behauptet in seiner 1936 für die Edition Eulenburg besorgten Ausgabe der Sinfonie, dass die Nr. 104 bei diesem Anlass erstmals in Wien erklang (übrigens spielte im selben Konzert Beethoven sein Zweites Klavierkonzert).

Das Hauptthema des Finale soll auf das kroatische Volkslied „Oj Jelena" zurückgehen, dessen erste zwölf Takte nachstehend angeführt werden und auf die sich die Ähnlichkeit auch beschränkt. Seinen Ursprung vermutete man ebenso in einem „London street cry" („Hot Cross Buns"[8] oder „Live Cod"), wofür es aber keinen Beleg gibt; die Nähe zur kroatischen Melodie lässt über die Herkunft des Themas wenig Zweifel.

Oj Jelena

Der Beiname „London" oder „Salomon" der eigentlich für alle zwölf letzten Sinfonien von Haydn gelten müsste, wird aus nicht bekannten Gründen nur mit diesem besonderen Werk verbunden.

Quellen

Partiturautograph: Staatsbibliothek zu Berlin - Preußischer Kulturbesitz, Musikabteilung Berlin . . . . AUT

Partiturabschrift eines Londoner Kopisten: British Library London . . . . LON

Handschriftliches Orchestermaterial, vermutlich von Johann Elßlers Hand (außer Vl. I/II): Fürstenbergisches Archiv Donaueschingen . . D/E

Gedruckte Orchesterstimmen von Birchall . . . . BIR

Birchalls Ausgabe von Salomons Arrangement für Quintett SAL5

Harry Newstone

8 a.a.O., Band II, S. 614f

Textual Notes

Str. = Strings
Br. = Brass
Ww. = Woodwind
a/h = another hand (in some cases Haydn or Salomon)
b(b) = bar(s)
n(n) = note(s)

Mov. I

bar 1 Str. *ff*, Winds, Timp. *f* in AUT; LON ditto but Fg. *ff*; D/E as AUT but Cor., Tr. 2 *ff*; BIR all parts *f*. The figure ♩.. ♬ shown correctly in AUT, BIR; LON, D/E sometimes ♩. ♪ (SAL5 ♩. ♪ throughout introduction).

3 Vl. I AUT *fz* written later over original *p* and *p* added to quavers – these dynamics added to bb4, 5; LON, BIR have original AUT reading (*p* b3, nothing bb4, 5); D/E as AUT changed reading, so Vl. I at least was copied after Haydn had added the new dynamics (possibly near the end of his London stay or after his return to Vienna, August 1795.)

7 Str. *ff* from LON, D/E; Vl. I, Vc/Cb. AUT *ff*; all parts BIR *f*

11 Vl. I n3 D/E altered (a/h) from g′ to f′, no doubt on basis of bb9, 10

12 Vla. LON slur over whole bar; BIR Vl. II, Vla. nn1–2 only slurred, Fl. nn2–3 only slurred, Cb. full bar rest

15, 16 Fg. slur from BIR

16a Fg., Str. AUT originally full bar (semibreve) rest, changed by Haydn to crotchet rest and added to other parts. Crotchet rest is in all sources; BIR adds fermata.

18 Vl. I/II BIR phrased 𝅗𝅥 ♫♫ but b26 𝅗𝅥 ♫♫ ; BIR quaver slur also bb66 (Fl., Vl. I), 74 (Ob. 1, Vl. I), 194 (Vl. I), 202 (Ob. 1), 251 (Fl., Vl. I)

31 Vl. I/II phrasing from BIR; Fl. D/E (a/h) this phrasing added to b207

32 Vl. I slur from LON, D/E; AUT merest hint of slur; LON b34 slur also (AUT, D/E nothing); AUT, LON slur generally clearer bb208, 210 (BIR slur only in Vl. I b210). On these bases we have added slur to all parallel parts.

33, 35–39 Vl. I/II stacc. dots from BIR analogous bb209, 211–215 (AUT in Vl. I b213 only); we also add them to Fl., Fg.

33, 35 Timp. minim in AUT, D/E as bb209, 211; LON, BIR crotchet

37 Ob. 1/2 follows BIR; AUT, LON, D/E  but b213  (also BIR)

44 Vl. I AUT nn1–2, 5–6 slur, reproduced  in LON, BIR (and SAL5) (D/E ); see also bb220–225

40, 216, 218 Fl., Ob. slur from AUT, BIR bb42, 218. These slurs could also apply to Vl. I, Vc/Cb. as shown in Vl. I D/E bb40 (a/h), 42 (original copyist hand).

47–50 Fl. BIR  etc.

58 Fl., Ob., Cl. phrasing from BIR where Vl. I slur includes n2 bb57, 59 (but not in Ww., Vla.); D/E slur elongated (a/h) to include n2 b57, this phrasing applied (a/h) to Cl. 2 and (a/h) both parts bb59–60. Ob. slurs bb58, 60 D/E (a/h).

58–60 Cl. 1/2 LON, BIR  each f♯″ changed in LON (a/h) from e″ and so printed in BIR

61, 63 Vl. I BIR n1 stacc. dot

66 Vla. AUT, LON, D/E minim, BIR adds dot (as Vl. II, Vc/Cb.). SAL5 dotted minim without tie from b65.

71 Fl., Vl. I phrasing from b23; BIR  (as b31)

74, 75 Vc. BIR slur extends over both bars

78 Fl. phrasing purely editorial; Vl. II nn3, 4 from BIR. Vla. n2–b79 slur from BIR, D/E (a/h).

79 Fl. nn2–3 slur from BIR. Ob., Vl. I (and bb115, 256 Fl., Vl. I) n2 BIR crotchet grace note, we follow quaver grace note of other sources.

80 Vl. I/II nn1–4 phrasing from BIR (also D/E a/h)

83, 84 Vl. I SAL5 phrasing ; ditto b85 where other sources have 

86 Vla., Vc/Cb. LON *fz*, others *f*; Str. already *f* from b80

91 All slurs from BIR

92 Cl. LON crotchet rest missing (hence BIR, whose engraver evidently thought the dot missing, 𝅗𝅥. 𝅘𝅥, a clear indication of the connection between LON and BIR, either directly or via an intermediate set of parts copied from LON, now lost)

92–94 LON (a/h?) n2 Fg., Vl. II *fz*, Vl. I *f*; BIR adds *fz* (sometimes written *rf* or *sf*) to Ww., Vla., also in bb95, 96 to Fl., Ob., Vl. I/II and b96 to Cl., Vla. (as in our text).

97–99 Cor. as Tr. LON, BIR with Cor. pedal starting at b100 and continuing to b104 (minim); believed to be copyist error in LON. Cor. 1/2 bb96–98 AUT rather faint as though Haydn had attempted to erase them with a fresh entry at the pedal at b99 (see b266). Conversely, these bars may have been added later – if the staves were originally blank the LON copyist could have assumed they were to read as Tr., but that does not explain either the faintness of the Cor. part or the displacement of the pedal.

99 Cl. 2 AUT originally a′ corrected by Haydn to g′ (or c″ – not clear); LON, D/E a′; BIR c″

103 Vla. LON, BIR nn3, 4 stacc.

109 Vl. II BIR n4 a′; this change also in SAL5

111 Ob., Vl. I/II BIR slur over nn3–4 only

112, 113 There is disagreement in the sources about the placing of *fz* in b112 (Vl. II, Vla.) and the length of slur (Cl., Fg.) in bb113, 114. Fl. slur (nn2–3) from BIR, added editorially to Vl. II; could apply also to Vla.

116, 117 Vc/Cb. AUT *fz* added to Ww., Vla. in LON, BIR; Cor., Tr. phrasing from BIR. Cl. 2 b117 n1 c″ (as Cl. 1), error perhaps occasioned by Haydn starting to write Cl. 2 here at concert pitch and crossing out the mistake.

135–136 Ob. slur from BIR

137 Vl. I nn1–4 phrasing from AUT; nn5–8 stacc. from LON, BIR. BIR continues this pattern for Vl. II bb139–144.

138 Ob. AUT stave empty (both oboes on one stave); LON (separate staves) d♯″ (as b137) for Ob. 1 only but a/h (Salomon?). D/E follows AUT literally, presuming b137 to be for Ob. 1 only. BIR assumes (we think correctly) Ob. 1/2 play in b137 and that Haydn simply forgot to write the d♯″ into b138.

140–141, 142–143 Vl. I slur across barline from BIR (also SAL5)

143–144 Cl. slur across barline from BIR

145 Vl. I LON, BIR nn1–4 slur; Vl. I/II, Vla. BIR n1 *p*

147, 151 Vl. I slur from BIR (SAL5 b147)

155 Vl. I AUT , reproduced LON as , D/E as ; BIR Vl. I , Vl. II ; SAL5 Vl. I, partly in Vl. II

166 Ob. AUT slur over nn1–4, presumably meant to continue; we add it to Fl. on this basis. Fl., Ob. BIR , also Vl. I bb166–173 (AUT nothing, perhaps Ob. phrasing meant to apply also to Vl. I); SAL5 nothing until bb172, 173 where Vl. I has

172 AUT, LON, D/E Vl. II alone *ff* for the harmonically pivotal e♯′(″); BIR adds *ff* to Ob. 1/2, *f* to Fl. (perhaps meant to be *ff*)

173 Fl. BIR slur could apply to Cl. 1; Cl. 2 n1 f″ (as Cl. 1)

175, 176, 177 Ww., Vl. I *fz* from LON, BIR, which applies it also to Fl., Ob., Fg. (not b177); Fl., Vl. I/II SAL5 *fz*

179–183 Vl. I BIR (b183 no stacc.). Fl. b181 slur possible on basis of b166.

184 Cl. 2 LON d″ written as tied minims instead of semibreve, so engraved in BIR

186, 187 Fg. slur on basis of Ob. slur in AUT, LON, D/E; Ob., Fg. BIR slur only within b186

188 Fl., Vl. I/II, Vla. phrasing from Vl. II AUT, LON, D/E, applied by BIR also to Fl., Vl. I, Vla.

189 Timp. LON, BIR have additional *f*

192 Tr. AUT stem thick at top which LON copyist reads as Tr. 1 d″; so reproduced in BIR

202 Fl. slur D/E a/h; also in SAL5 Vl. I as Fl. cue but not in Fl. part itself!

204 Ob. phrasing from D/E (a/h), reproduced in BIR but without nn1–2 slur in Ob. 2 (which is above Ob. 1 here)

207 Fl. phrasing from D/E (a/h) consistent with BIR Vl. I/II b31; Ob. stacc. from D/E

208 Vl. II, Vla., Vc/Cb. LON *ff*, Cl., Vl. I *for.*

220–223 Vl. I BIR  , bb224, 225  ; we follow phrasing of bb44, 45

228–231 Fg. BIR  , bb232, 233  , ditto Vc/Cb. except bb228, 229 have 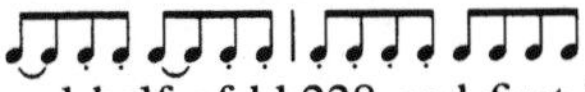 (i.e. phrasings for second half of bb228 and first half of b229 have been transposed)

254, 255 Fl., Vl. I LON, BIR slur over both bars

255 Vl. II nn3–4 slur from b78

257–259 Fl., Ob., Cl., Vl. I/II quaver phrasing from BIR

257, 263, 264 Timp. AUT e, a curious error copied into LON (b257 only) but corrected in other sources

262 Tr. minim from BIR; AUT crotchet (LON Tr. 1 minim, Tr. 2 crotchet!)

264 Vla. BIR  , no other source has the b; Vla. AUT 'col Basso'

270 Cor. AUT empty bar (D/E rest); pedal extended into this bar LON a/h, but semibreve or minim unclear; Cor. 1 minim, Cor. 2 semibreve BIR! See b103.

281 Fg., Vc/Cb. BIR

284 Vl. I AUT slur of uncertain length from n1 which LON (and D/E Vl. I) read as  ; BIR bb284, 285 Str.,  (SAL5 no phrasing)

276 Fg. LON Tutti, probably should apply to b277; not in AUT but in BIR, also D/E where it is crossed out and replaced by bar rest

Mov. II

bar 3, 19, 76 Vla. nn4–5 slur from BIR

12 Vl. I/II n3 stacc. dot from LON, BIR (and SAL5)

13–14, 94–95 Vla., Vc/Cb. BIR quavers slurred across barline

16 Vl. I BIR nn3, 4 stacc.

17, 21 Fg. BIR  (ditto LON b21); Fg. b17, Ob. bb60–63 AUT (ditto LON, D/E)

17–25 Fl. AUT originally octave above Vl. I, and bb26–37 as Vl. I, but crossed out by Haydn. Fg. bb17, 21 phrase as Vl. I; Fg. b21 AUT nn2–4 slur reproduced in D/E, later crossed out (a/h). Str. b25 BIR *p* here instead of b26.

32 Vl. I AUT, D/E slur does not reach to end of bar; LON, SAL5 have whole-bar slur, probably Haydn's intention. BIR and Vl. II nn1–2 slur (nn3–4 slur missing?); SAL5 Vl. II .

42, 44, 46 Vl. I and b43 slurs from BIR; Ob. 1/2, Cl. AUT no dynamic at b42 (our *f* from BIR) but Ob. 1/2 *ff* at b43 (Fl. *f* here in AUT but *ff* probably intended).

43, 45 Fl., Ob. 1/2 phrasing from BIR (also SAL5 Fl.); Cl. 2 b43 slur from BIR which we add to Fg. (matching Vl. I)

46 It appears from AUT that Haydn at first continued to write D-minor harmony for the first half of this bar, then changed n2 Vc/Cb. from a to b♭ but forgot to make the same change for Vl. II n3; the Vc/Cb. correction is in LON, D/E and the Vl. II correction (a′ to b♭′) visible in LON but D/E Vl. II still has the a′.

47 Vl. I BIR nn1–2 no tie; nn7–8 slur editorial suggestion

50 Vla. AUT upper notes e♭′, all other sources c′

54, 55 Fl., Ob. LON slurred mostly in pairs, ditto BIR Fl. but Ob. whole-bar slurs; Ww. b55 last note stacc/accent from AUT, D/E; LON has these only in Ob., BIR only in Fg; Vl. I n16 stacc/accent AUT only.

59 Str. BIR nn2–4 stacc., no phrasing other sources except SAL5 Vla. where nn2–4 are slurred

60 Cor. 2 LON, BIR g (not g′) as b64

60, 61 Ob. 1 tie across barline from AUT, LON, D/E, probably meant to apply also to bb62–63, Ob. 2 bb61–62, 63–64. These are not in BIR where bb60, 62, 64 nn3, 4 are stacc. Ob. 1 bb61, 63, Ob. 2 bb62, 64 nn1–2 slurs from BIR also D/E (a/h) which continues Ob. slurs in bb65, 66.

65, 66 Fg., Vl. II, Vla., Vc/Cb. phrasing from BIR (and SAL5 Vl. II, Vla.); other sources only Fl., Ob. 1, Vl. I have this phrasing

67 Cor. 2 BIR octave lower, Fl., Ob. stacc.

68, 69 Tr. 2 D/E altered (a/h) to ; in no other source but possible for Tr., Cor.

70 Ob. 1/2 as AUT; Ob. 1/2 LON crotchet, Fg., Vl. II, Vla., Vc/Cb. BIR quaver. Vl. I BIR b70 *f*, b71 *decres:*, b73 *p*.

73, 74 Fg. dynamics and stacc. from BIR

75 Fl., Fg. n1 crotchet in all sources, changed here to quaver on basis of Str.

85 Vla. n1 from AUT, D/E; LON bar rest(!) which may account for BIR having d′

88 Cor. 2 LON, BIR nn4, 5 as Cor. 1 and nn6–8 g′

89 Tr. 2 LON, BIR nn2, 4 as Tr. 1; n5 stacc. from BIR most parts

92 Vla. BIR *p* instead of *fz*

97 Vl. I nn1–2 slur as BIR (AUT b16 though BIR here nn3, 4 stacc.); AUT nn1–3 slur, so copied into D/E; LON nn1–2 slur

98–100 Fl., Vl. I/II nn3–8 slur from BIR (also D/E a/h although slurs in bb98, 99 Vl. I have been crossed out); b100 Vl. I BIR *p* under n1 (nothing in Fl.)

101 Fl., Vl. I stacc. dots from BIR, added to Vl. II

106ff. The original version of this passage is shown in the Appendix (p. 102). AUT shows that after fermata bar Haydn intended to continue with a modulating string passage of which he only partly wrote the Vl. I part before scratching it out and replacing it with the Ww. passage of the final version (now b114ff.).

107 Vl. I AUT, LON, D/E nn1, 2 ♪. ♬ , BIR ♪.. ♬

110 Str. BIR *ff* beat 2 and ——— from beginning of b111

114–115, 116–117 Fg. slur across barline from BIR

122 Ob. 1, Timp. BIR *f*

122–123 Cor. LON, BIR no slur

124 Fg., Str. AUT originally *p* on beat 2, crossed out by Haydn

125 Cor. 1 AUT, LON, D/E nn1, 2 ♪. ♬, correct in BIR; Fl. slur, stacc. applied editorially

126, 127 Fl., Ob. 1, Fg., Vl. I AUT difficult to tell whether 2- or 4-note slurs. BIR has 4-note slur in Ob. 1 b126, two 2-note slurs in Fl., Fg., Vl. I in both bars and Ob. 1 b127, which phrasing we follow; LON Vl. I both bars, Ob. 1 b126 nn3, 4 stacc. dots. Vc/Cb. b126 slur from LON, BIR, ditto Vla. slur bb126–127.

127–130 Vl. I phrasing from BIR

131 Fl. phrasing from BIR (also D/E a/h); AUT has two tiny triplet slurs beginning of bar, reproduced in LON as [music notation: three quavers with triplet slur] ; SAL5 no phrasing. Only BIR has dynamic (*p*) here; LON *p* at b132 (also SAL5), another at b133 and *f* at b134. D/E written with repeat mark and 'bis' with added instruction '1° *pia*, 2do *for*', all, it seems, in the original copyist's hand. In AUT the Fl. *p* b133 and *for* b134 do not appear to be in Haydn's hand; this *for* not in BIR.

135 Tr. AUT d″ corrected to c″ in LON, BIR; the correction also in D/E (a/h) but as crotchet and with Tr. 2 an octave below Tr. 1

137 Vl. I AUT n1 lower note possibly g′; LON, BIR, SAL5 g′, D/E a′. Fl. all sources crotchet which we adjust to dotted crotchet (as Ob. 1, Vl. I).

140 Vl. I/II slurs from BIR

141 Vl. II LON, SAL5 n4 quaver rest (AUT [music notation]); n4 d′ in D/E, BIR. Vla. slur from BIR (D/E a/h).

148 Fg. 1, Vla. slur to b149 from BIR

149 Cor. *pp* from BIR

150 Cor. 2 n1 e′ as b149 (AUT, LON, D/E c′); Vl. I BIR n2 a′; Vl. II SAL5 nn2, 3 [music notation]

151, 152 Stacc. dots not in AUT but in D/E Fl. as a correction in what looks like Haydn's hand, as well as in many of the LON, BIR parts; we have added them to all parts

Mov. III

No dynamic to begin except BIR Fl. upbeat (only) *fz* which we adjust to *f*

bar 1 Ob. 2, Cl. 1/2, Fg., Cor., Timp., Vc/Cb. BIR *f*

5 Fg., Vc/Cb. slur from LON (added later?) which we apply to b13 (possible for Fl.), b39; slur also in SAL5 bb5, 6, 13, 14

6 Cl. 2 as Cl. 1 in LON, BIR

7 Cl. 2 AUT no *tr* but in LON, D/E, BIR. Tr. 1 AUT *tr* looks crossed out; in LON not BIR, originally in D/E (also Tr. 2) but erased; Cor. 1 *tr* in AUT, LON, originally in D/E

(also Cor. 2) but crossed out; Cor. BIR no *tr*; Vc/Cb. (Fg.) LON *tr*; Cor. 2 D/E *tr* b15 but crossed out; Cor. 2, Tr. 2 *tr* unplayable at the time on natural instruments

9ff. All parts BIR *pp* from last beat of b8

17–19 *fz* and Ww. slurs across barline from BIR; ditto bb35–37 (added editorially to Ob. bb37–38 and Cl. 1/2 bb35–36)

19 Vla. n2 b from BIR (other sources f♯′ making parallel fifths with Vc/Cb.)

20–24 Fl., Ob., Fg., Vla., Vc/Cb. quaver slurs from BIR, also Fl., Ob., Vl. II phrasing bb22–25, Tr. 1 tie bb25, 26

34–40 Fl., Vl. I, Vla. quaver slurs (from b34 beat 3) from BIR, partly in D/E (a/h)

39 Fl., Ob. 1, Vl. I nn2–3 slur from BIR (but missing in Vla.), D/E Ob. 1 (a/h)

40 Vc/Cb. *fz* from BIR; LON Vl. II n2 *for* (not in BIR)

43 Ob. 1/2, Fg., Vla., Vc/Cb. BIR n1 *fz*

44 Fl., Ob., Vl. I/II D/E (a/h) n2 *fp*, also SAL5 Fl., Vl. II

47, 48 All parts except Vl. I/II D/E (a/h) (also SAL5 all parts)

49 Fl., Fg. BIR n1 *fz*

58 Ob. 1 AUT marked 'col Violino 1°' to double bar and so copied into D/E but then crossed out from last quaver of b58; this change in LON, i.e., last note replaced by quaver rest and five bars rest follow; BIR so engraved

61–71, *et seq.* Phrasing from BIR, ditto Vl. I bb72 (Fg. b71)–78, Vl. II, Vc/Cb. bb75–77 (Vl. II AUT slur within bar); AUT no phrasing (or LON from b62); Ob. 2 bb74–75 slur from SAL5 Fl.

77 Vl. II LON n1 b♭, error reproduced in BIR

79 Vl. II all sources follow AUT in placing slur within bar, we adjust to read as b53, similarly at b89

80–86 Ob. 1, Vl. I BIR phrased

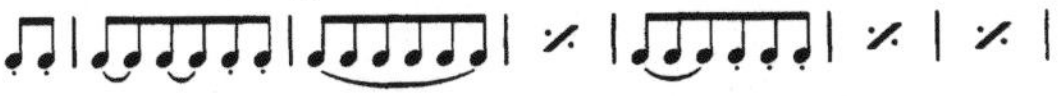

(no phrasing AUT bb84–86, SAL5 has whole-bar slurs)

84–87 Fl. slur from BIR (SAL5 has slur over bb85–86)

95–99 Vl. I AUT slur length unclear, LON, D/E exclude upbeat to b95 but BIR phrases Ob. 1/2, Vl. I across barline as before; Ob. b95 AUT slur only within bar but perhaps meant to be similar to Vl. I

95–104 Ob. 1/2, Vl. I (bb100–103), Vl. II (b101, 103) slurs from BIR

103 Ob. 2 AUT originally dotted minim e″ altered to present reading; LON has the correction (a/h, Haydn?) and is in BIR, not D/E

Mov. IV

bar 2–3 Cor., Vc. BIR no tie, ditto LON Cor.

12, 16 Vla., Vc/Cb. LON, BIR slur does not include bb11, 15

13, 197, 201 Vl. II BIR ; b17 as other sources

14 Vc. AUT minims slurred, error carried into LON, D/E, not BIR

17, 18 Vla. slur added on basis of bb201–202 (all sources), possible for Vc.

24 Vl. AUT phrasing stops middle of bar (ditto LON, D/E), BIR continues to b28 as in our text

28 Fg., Vla., Vc/Cb. stacc. on basis of Vl. I/II

29 All parts except Cor., Tr., Timp. *ff* from BIR (nothing in Vc/Cb.)

31, 37 Fl. slur from BIR

33–34 Ob. 1 BIR no tie

36 Phrasing from AUT which has slur over nn1–2(3?) in Vl. II only, with stacc. on n4

37 Vla. phrasing and *fz* from SAL5

42 This bar comes after a page turn in AUT where Timp. (a/h) has minim followed by minim rest; this reading in LON, BIR but D/E bb42–44 has in original copyist's hand. We follow this logical continuation (with reservations about the last note).

43 Cor. 2 LON, BIR n2 c″

45/46, 49/50 (and bb156/157, 160/161, 233/234, 237/238) Ww., Br. BIR slurs mostly replaced by stacc. minims; in these places and at bb51/52, 158/159, 235/236 BIR Vla., Vc/Cb. slur or tie across barline, ditto Vc/Cb. bb47/48, 162/163

52ff. Fl., Ob., Vl. I BIR n1 *p*, other parts *p* at b54(–64) with many reminders, especially after *fz* which BIR adds to Vl. I (n1) bb55, 56, 59, 60

54, 55 Vl. II AUT very faint (erased?) tie, omitted in other sources

55, 56, 59, 60 Ob. 2 BIR no tie; Vla. slur across barline (g♯′–a′) and stacc. bb56, 60 also BIR

64 Vl. II BIR, D/E (a/h)

73–75 Fg., Str. BIR quavers slurred in fours, bb76–80 whole-bar slurs; some of these slurs in D/E (a/h), see also b240ff.

77–81 Cb. BIR octave lower (to n1 b81)

83 Cl. 1/2 from BIR; AUT, D/E rest, LON originally so but Cl. 1 has g″ added a/h (Haydn?), nothing in Cl. 2.

87–89 Vl. II LON originally as other sources but notes crossed out and altered (a/h) to (i.e., doubling Fg. instead of Vla.)

87ff., 168ff., 247ff. Phrasing unclear in AUT and conflicting in sources; we follow them where possible and in accordance with the melodic needs and for the *fz* to be effective

97 Vl. I/II slur carried over to b98 on basis of AUT bb260–261 Fl., Vl. I; Fg., Vc/Cb. editorial slur suggested both places

109–119a All quaver slurs from BIR (and LON Vl. I/II 119a only)

114 Fl., Ob. 2 n2 from BIR; AUT, LON, D/E respectively b″ and b′ minim

123, 124 Ob. 2 d in AUT only, all other sources rest; if LON copyist saw only the empty stave above the note it would explain the two bars rest here and in BIR, but it is less easy to account for the note's absence in D/E unless it was written into AUT after D/E was copied, but the appearance of the score does not support this

126 Tr. 1/2 crotchet as LON, BIR (and Cor. 1/2); AUT, D/E minim

131 Fl. slur suggested from SAL5

132 Tr. 1 LON (a/h) f″; so engraved in BIR Tr. 1 (and Cor. 1 with tie from b131)

137 Vl. I BIR, D/E (a/h) ♩♩♩♩ ♩ ♩ (nn1–4 slur also in SAL5)

137, 138 Cor. BIR 𝅗𝅥 𝅗𝅥 | 𝅗𝅥 𝅗𝅥

139, 148 Str. BIR quavers slurred in fours (except Vl. I b139 nn1–4, ♩♩♩♩)

147, 148 Cl. 1/2 AUT (written separately at end of score) missing, corrected in D/E. LON, BIR bb147–150 rest.

153 Cl. 1/2 LON, BIR slur to b154; Vla. AUT d′, corrected LON, D/E, BIR to e′

162 Ww. slur to b163 from BIR (so in SAL5 Fl.)

167–192 Phrasing mostly from BIR with some slurs from LON (Vl. II bb179, 180)

198 Vl. I/II, Vla. n2 ' (stacc.) on basis of b6; BIR n2 Vl. I/II, Vla. >, Vc. ' (stacc.)

203, 204 Fg. 1/2 from BIR; all other sources rest. If Haydn was allowing Fg. to rest after eight-bar pedal (Cor. 1/2 here have four bars rest after pedal) it is curious that he did not do so at b19ff.

208 Ob. 2 n3 all sources f♯″ except BIR with a′ (as b24); Timp. LON seems to have got a bar out here resulting in minim rest second half of bar in BIR; LON bb209, 210 corrected a/h (Haydn?), our reading from AUT

210 Ob. 2 AUT n3 missing (empty space after crotchet rest) which other sources change to minim rest; we suggest Haydn forgot to write in the d″ and that at the end of the bar Ob. 2 should read as Ob. 1

218 Vl. I n4 AUT, D/E c♯‴; LON c♯‴ changed to d‴ or vice-versa, BIR, SAL5 d‴. Cl. 1, Cor. 2 tie to b219 from BIR which, however, does not have the Fl. tie here.

221, 222, 225, 226 Vl. I BIR n2 >

223 Cl. 2 LON n1 b♭′, Vl. I BIR ♩♩♩♩ (and at b227, also Cl. 1/2, Vl. II bb313, 317) but we suggest four-note slur as AUT bb57, 61, 63

231 Cl. 1/2 n2 all sources show as minim rest, but see b43 which process we follow here

234 Fl., Fg. all sources crotchet, also LON Ob. 1/2 at first but changed (with Fl., Fg.) to minim

240–243 Fg., Str. BIR nn1–8 slurred

248 Fl. *p* from BIR

266–271 Fl. as Vl. I LON, D/E, BIR with g♯″ tied from b265, then (tie from BIR)

274 Vla. nn3–4 slur from BIR

287–292 Str. BIR quavers inconsistently slurred by whole or half bar

293, 294 Fl., Fg., Str. BIR nn3–4 slurred (also D/E, Vl. I/II, Vla. a/h)

295–300 Fl., Fg., Str. BIR crotchets stacc.

301 Fl., Ob. 1, Fg., Str., except Vla., BIR *ff*

303, 304 Omitted in LON so copyist wrote 'bis' over bb301–302 not noticing that in b304 Haydn had written e″ for Cl. 1 instead of g″ as in b302; BIR follows LON

308 Cl. 2 LON, BIR n2 g′

309 General *ff* from BIR (except Fl., Cl., Timp.); note subtle drop to *f* in Cor. b311 (BIR only) which could also apply to Tr. and possibly Timp.

309ff. Cor. 2 LON e′ changed a/h to c′ (the alteration marked 'NB') and this long note held for one bar too many in both Cor. ending (with minim) in b319 instead of b318. LON b319 is omitted; the Cor. 2 change, the extra held bar, and the omission of b319 are all in BIR.

311 Fl. D/E marked *8va* and at b330 (after n1) *loco*, both a/h

311–318 Vc. doubling of Vla. missing in LON, BIR (i.e., Vc. = Cb.) and it has been crossed through in D/E (a/h). Fg. 2 LON altered (a/h) from long held F♯ to . This change, which is also in BIR, and that to Cor. 2 b309, was obviously made to avoid the bold clash of tonic and dominant harmonies in this passage, but Haydn numbered the first few bars of the D-major pedal chord in Fg., Cor., Timp., Vc/Cb. as though to ensure this harmony was to be held. One is reminded of a similar (if gentler) clash between solo Fl. and Str. in the Trio of the 'Clock' Symphony (bb86, 87) and its subsequent 'correction' by other hands.

314 Ob. 2 as LON (a/h?), BIR; AUT bar rest; D/E observes bar rest and crosses out a″ in Ob. 1

324 Ww., Vla., Vc/Cb. *fz* from BIR (D/E a/h has *sf*)

325 Vl. I BIR reads as b321

326 Cl. AUT surplus bar (minim f″) which is crossed out in LON, D/E and not shown in BIR

326 Fl., Ob., Str. BIR n1 *fz*, Vl. I n2 *ff*

333 General *ff* from BIR

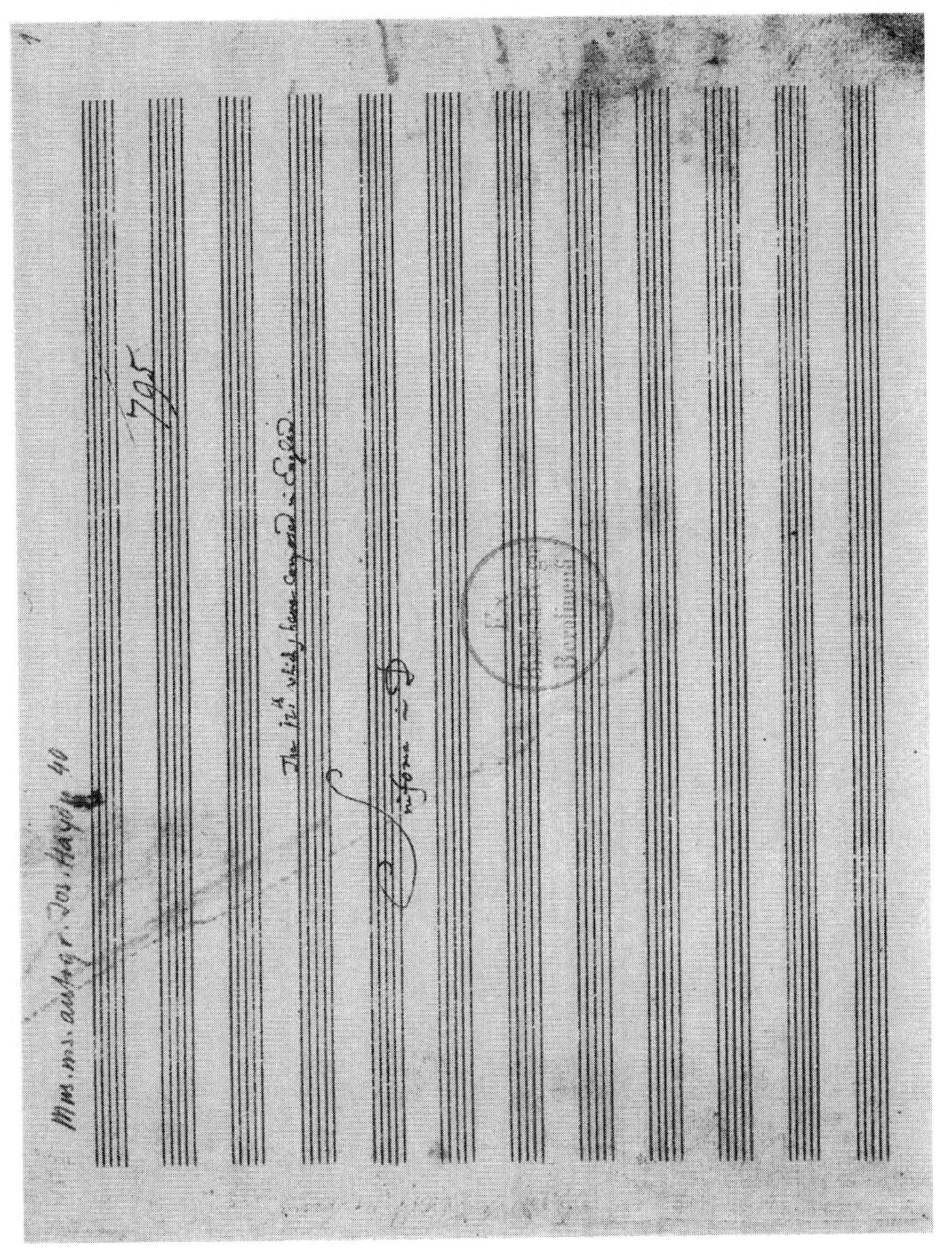

Haydn, Symphony No. 104, Autograph MS
D-B Mus.ms.autogr. Jos. Haydn 40, fol. 1r
Preußischer Kulturbesitz Berlin – Musikabteilung mit Mendelssohn-Archiv

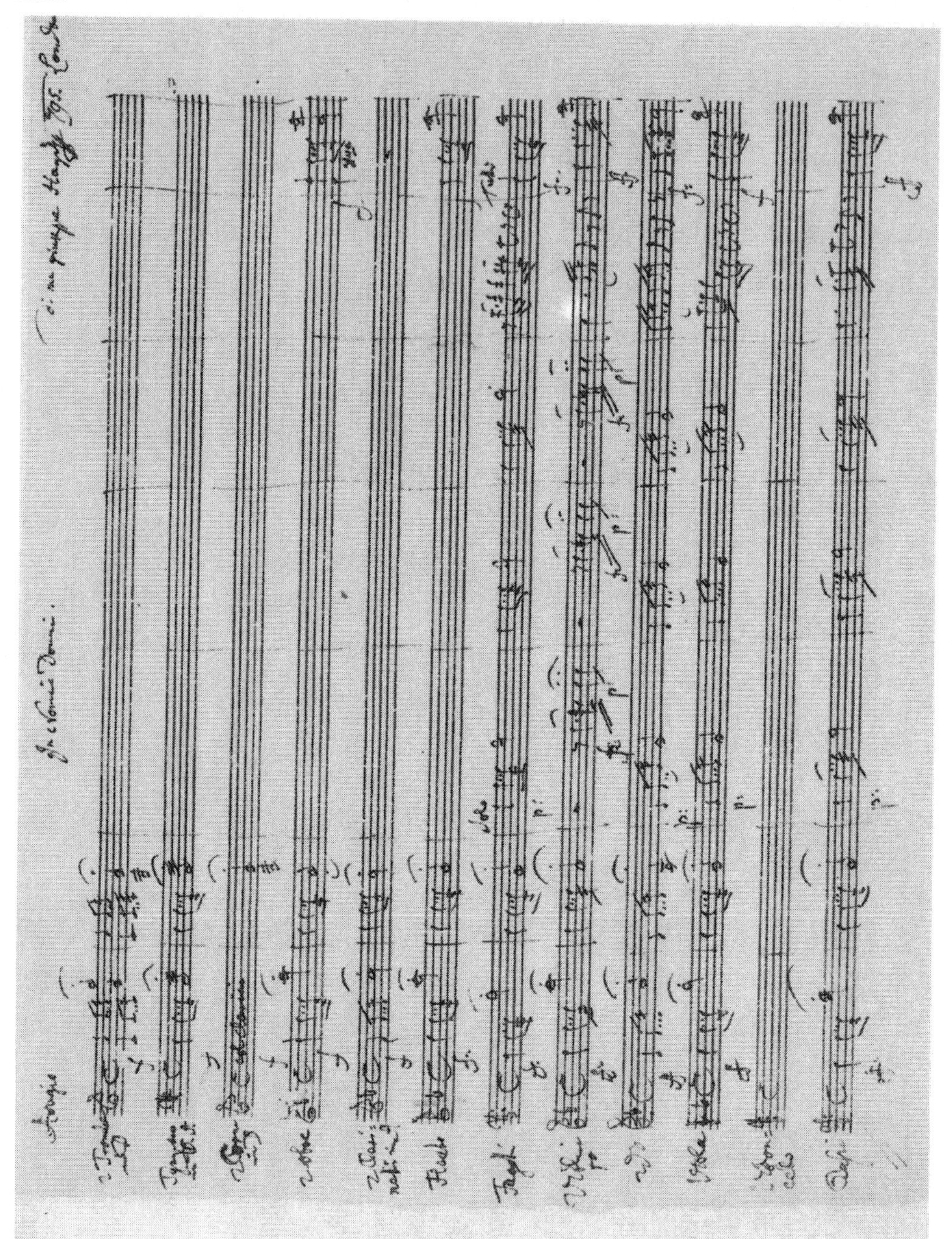

Haydn, Symphony No. 104, Autograph MS
D-B Mus.ms.autogr. Jos. Haydn 40, fol. 1v
Preußischer Kulturbesitz Berlin – Musikabteilung mit Mendelssohn-Archiv

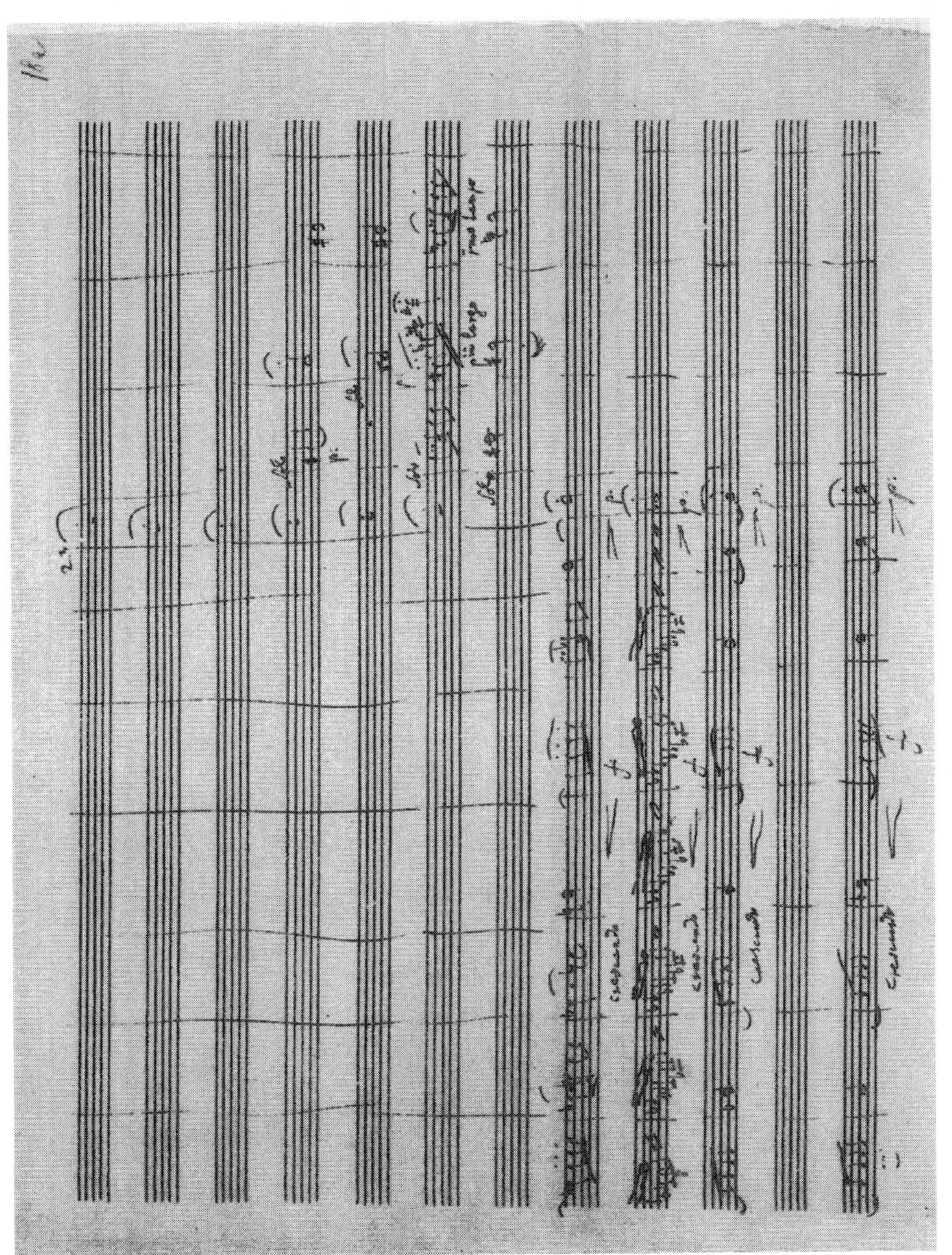

Haydn, Symphony No. 104, Autograph MS
D-B Mus.ms.autogr. Jos. Haydn 40, fol. 18a(r)
Preußischer Kulturbesitz Berlin – Musikabteilung mit Mendelssohn-Archiv

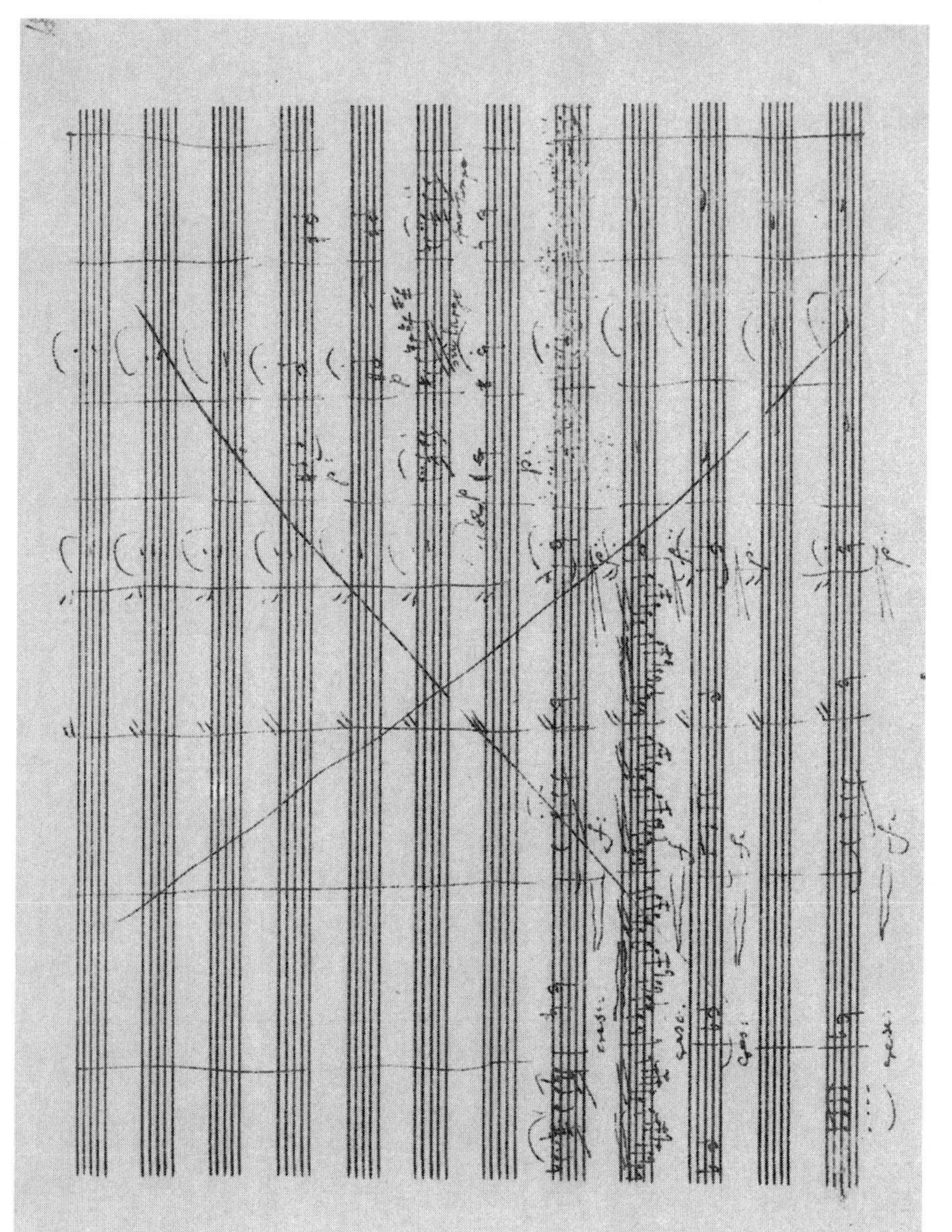

Haydn, Symphony No. 104, Autograph MS
D-B Mus.ms.autogr. Jos. Haydn 40, fol. 18r
Preußischer Kulturbesitz Berlin – Musikabteilung mit Mendelssohn-Archiv

SYMPHONY No. 104
'London'

In Nomine Domini

Joseph Haydn
(1732–1809)

Fl. 1 2
Ob. 1 2
Fg. 1 2
Vl. I II
Vla.
Vc. e Cb.
[a 2]
Tutti
Solo
Vc.

Fl. 1 2
Fg. 1 2
Vl. I II
Vla.
Vc. e Cb.
Solo
Vc.
Tutti

14
[a 2]
Fl. 1 2
Ob. 1 2
[Solo]
Cl. (A) 1 2
Fg. 1 2
Tutti
[Soli]
Cor. (D) 1 2
Tr. (D) 1 2
Timp. 1 2
I
Vl.
II
Vla.
Vc. e Cb.
Allegro
17
Solo
Fg. 1 2
I
Vl.
II
Vla.
Vc. e Cb.

22
Vl.
I
II
Vla.
Vc.
e Cb.
27
Vl.
I
II
Vla.
Vc.
e Cb.
[a 2]
32
Fl. 1 2
f
Ob. 1 2
Cl. (A) 1 2
Fg. 1 2
Tutti
Cor. (D) 1 2
Tr. (D) 1 2
Timp.
Vl.
I
II
Vla.
Vc.
e Cb.

37
[a 2]
Fl. 1 2
Ob. 1 2
Cl. (A) 1 2
[a 2]
Fg. 1 2
Cor. (D) 1 2
Tr. (D) 1 2
Timp.
I
Vl.
II
Vla.
Vc. e Cb.

42
[a 2]
Fl. 1 2
Ob. 1 2
a 2
Cl. (A) 1 2
a 2
[a 2]
Fg. 1 2
Cor. (D) 1 2
Tr. (D) 1 2
Timp.
I
Vl.
II
Vla.
Vc. e Cb.

47
[a 2]
Fl. 1 2
a 2
Ob. 1 2
a 2
Cl. (A) 1 2
[a 2]
Fg. 1 2
Cor. (D) 1 2
Tr. (D) 1 2
Timp.
I
Vl.
II
Vla.
Vc.
e Cb.

52
[a 2]
Fl. 1 2
Ob. 1 2
Cl. (A) 1 2
a 2
Fg. 1 2
Vl. I
II
Vla.
Vc. e Cb.
57
Cor. (D) 1 2
Tr. (D) 1 2

62
[a 2]
Fl. 1 2
Solo
p
a 2
Ob. 1 2
Solo
p
Cl. (A) 1 2
[a 2]
Fg. 1 2
a 2
Cor. (D) 1 2
a 2
Tr. (D) 1 2
I
Vl.
II
p
Vla.
p
Vc. e Cb.
p

68
1.
Fl. 1 2
1.
Ob. 1 2
Solo
Fg. 1 2
p

I
Vl.
II
Vla.
Vc. e Cb.

★) See Textual Notes/Siehe Einzelanmerkungen

86
[Tutti]
[a 2]
Fl. 1 2
Tutti
a 2
Ob. 1 2
Cl. (A) 1 2
Tutti
[a 2]
Fg. 1 2
Cor. (D) 1 2
a 2
Tr. (D) 1 2
Timp.
I
Vl.
II
Vla.
Vc. e Cb.

92
[a 2]
Fl. 1 2
fz
Ob. 1 2
a 2
Cl. (A) 1 2
Fg. 1 2
[a 2]
Cor. (D) 1 2
a 2
Tr.(D) 1 2
Timp.
I
Vl.
II
Vla.
Vc. e Cb.

98
[a 2]
Fl. 1 2
Solo
Ob. 1 2
Solo
Cl. (A) 1 2
[a 2]
Fg. 1 2
Solo
Cor. (D) 1 2
a 2
Tr. (D) 1 2
Timp.
I
Vl.
II
Vla.
Vc. e Cb.

105
Ob. 1 2
Fg. 1 2
Vl. I
II
Vla.
Vc. e Cb.
112
Fl. 1 2
Ob. 1 2
Tutti
a 2
Cl. (A) 1 2
Fg. 1 2
Cor. (D) 1 2
Tr. (D) 1 2
Timp.
Vl. I
II
Vla.
Vc. e Cb.

118 [a 2]
Fl. 1 2
a 2
Ob. 1 2
Cl. (A) 1 2
[a 2]
Fg. 1 2
Cor. (D) 1 2
Tr. (D) 1 2
Timp.
I
Vl.
II
Vla.
Vc. e Cb.

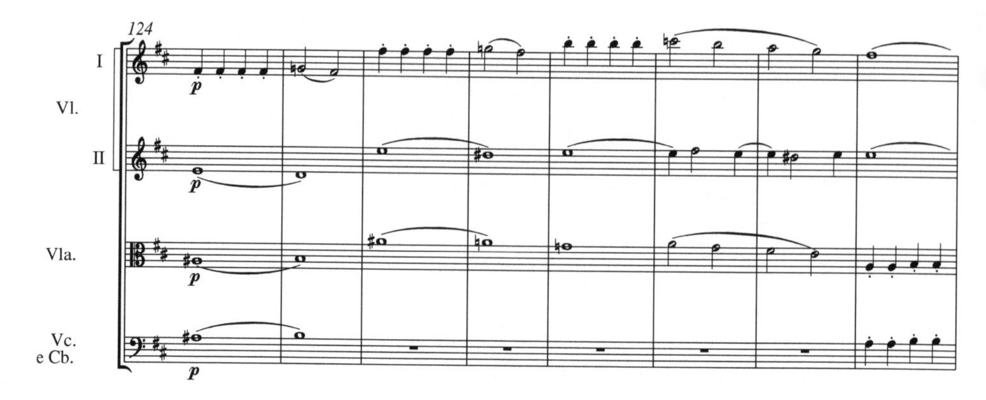
124
I
Vl.
II
Vla.
Vc.
e Cb.

132
Solo
Tutti
Fl. 1 2
Ob. 1 2
Cl. (A) 1 2
a 2
Fg. 1 2
[a 2]
Cor. (D) 1 2
Tr. (D) 1 2
I
Vl.
II
Vla.
Vc.
e Cb.

138
144
Fl.
Ob.
Cl. (A)
Fg.
Cor. (D)
Tr. (D)
Vl.
I
II
Vla.
Vc.
e Cb.
a 2
[a 2]
p

150
Fl. 1 2
Ob. 1 2
Cl. (A) 1 2
Fg. 1 2
Solo
p
f
[a 2]
Cor. (D) 1 2
a 2
Tr. (D) 1 2
a 2
Vl. I II
Vla.
Vc. e Cb.
156
[a 2]
[a 2]
a 2
a 2

162
[a 2]
Fl. 1 2
Ob. 1 2
a 2
Cl. (A) 1 2
[a 2]
Fg. 1 2
a 2
Cor. (D) 1 2
I
Vl.
II
Vla.
Vc. e Cb.
167
[a 2]
Fl. 1 2
a 2
Ob. 1 2
Cl. (A) 1 2
[a 2]
Fg. 1 2
a 2
Cor. (D) 1 2
I
Vl.
II
Vla.
Vc. e Cb.

172
[a 2]
Fl. 1 2
f
fz
Ob. 1 2
ff
Cl. (A) 1 2
[a 2]
Fg. 1 2
a 2
Cor. (D) 1 2
Tr. (D) 1 2
[f]
Timp.
I
Vl.
II
Vla.
Vc. e Cb.

178
[a 2]
Fl. 1 2
Ob. 1 2
a 2
Cl. (A) 1 2
Fg. 1 2
[a 2]
Cor. (D) 1 2
a 2
Tr. (D) 1 2
a 2
Timp.
I
Vl.
II
Vla.
Vc. e Cb.

184
[a 2]
Fl. 1 2
Ob. 1 2
Cl. (A) 1 2
[a 2]
Fg. 1 2
Cor. (D) 1 2
a 2
Tr. (D) 1 2
Timp.
I
Vl.
II
Vla.
Vc.
e Cb.

190
[a 2]
Fl. 1 2
Ob. 1 2
Cl. (A) 1 2
[a 2]
Solo
Fg. 1 2
p
Cor. (D) 1 2
a 2
Tr. (D) 1 2
Timp.
I
Vl.
II
p
p
Vla.
p
Vc. e Cb.
p

196
Fl. 1 2
Solo
Ob. 1 2
2. [Solo]
1. Solo
Vl. I II
Vla.
Vc. e Cb.
203
1.
2.
Cl. (A) 1 2
Fg. 1 2
Tutti
Cor. (D) 1 2
Tr. (D) 1 2
Timp.

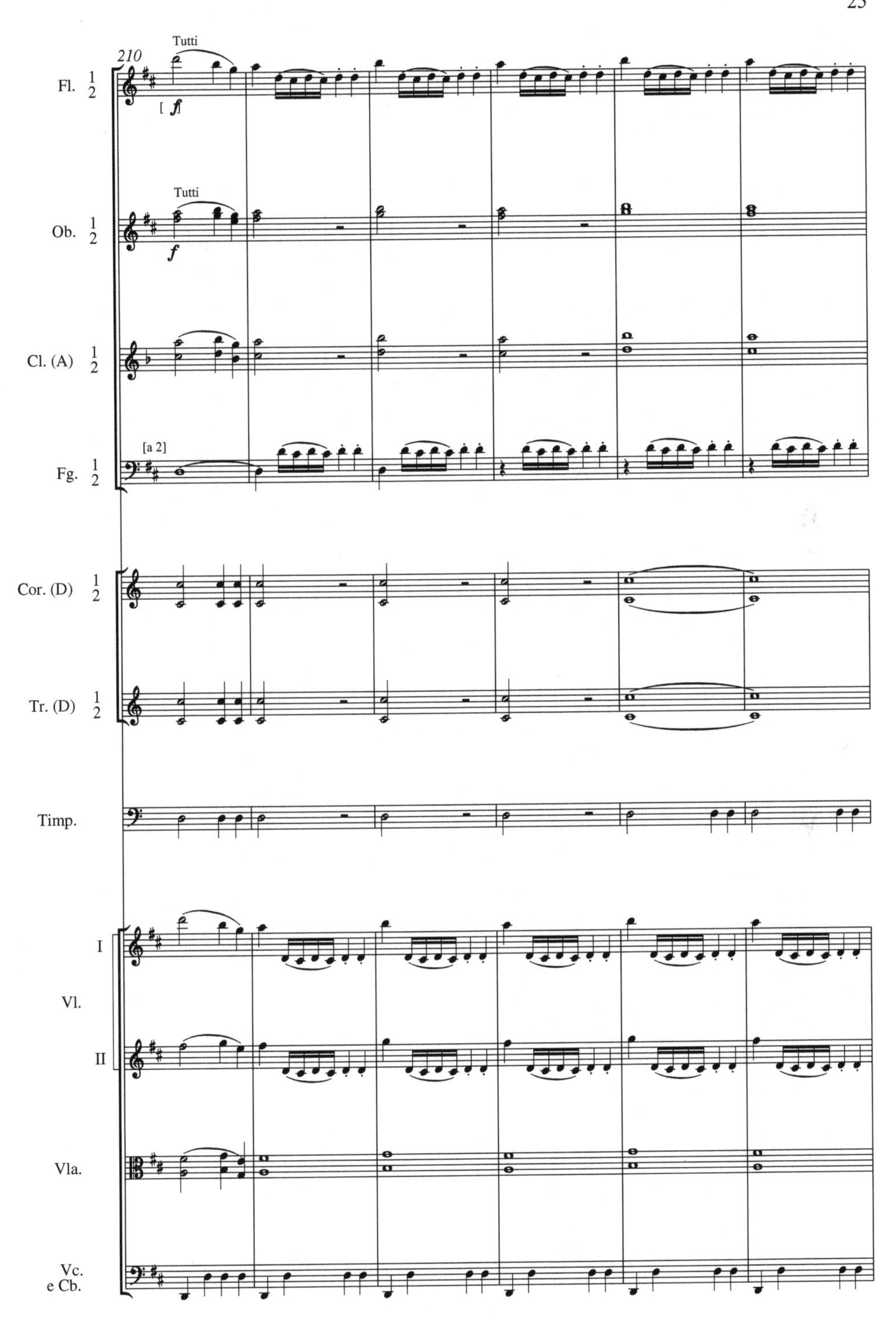
210
Tutti
Fl. 1 2
[f]
Tutti
Ob. 1 2
f
Cl. (A) 1 2
[a 2]
Fg. 1 2
Cor. (D) 1 2
Tr. (D) 1 2
Timp.
I
Vl.
II
Vla.
Vc. e Cb.

216
[a 2]
Fl. 1 2
Ob. 1 2
Cl. (A) 1 2
a 2
[a 2]
Fg. 1 2
Cor. (D) 1 2
Tr. (D) 1 2
Timp.
I
Vl.
II
Vla.
Vc.
e Cb.

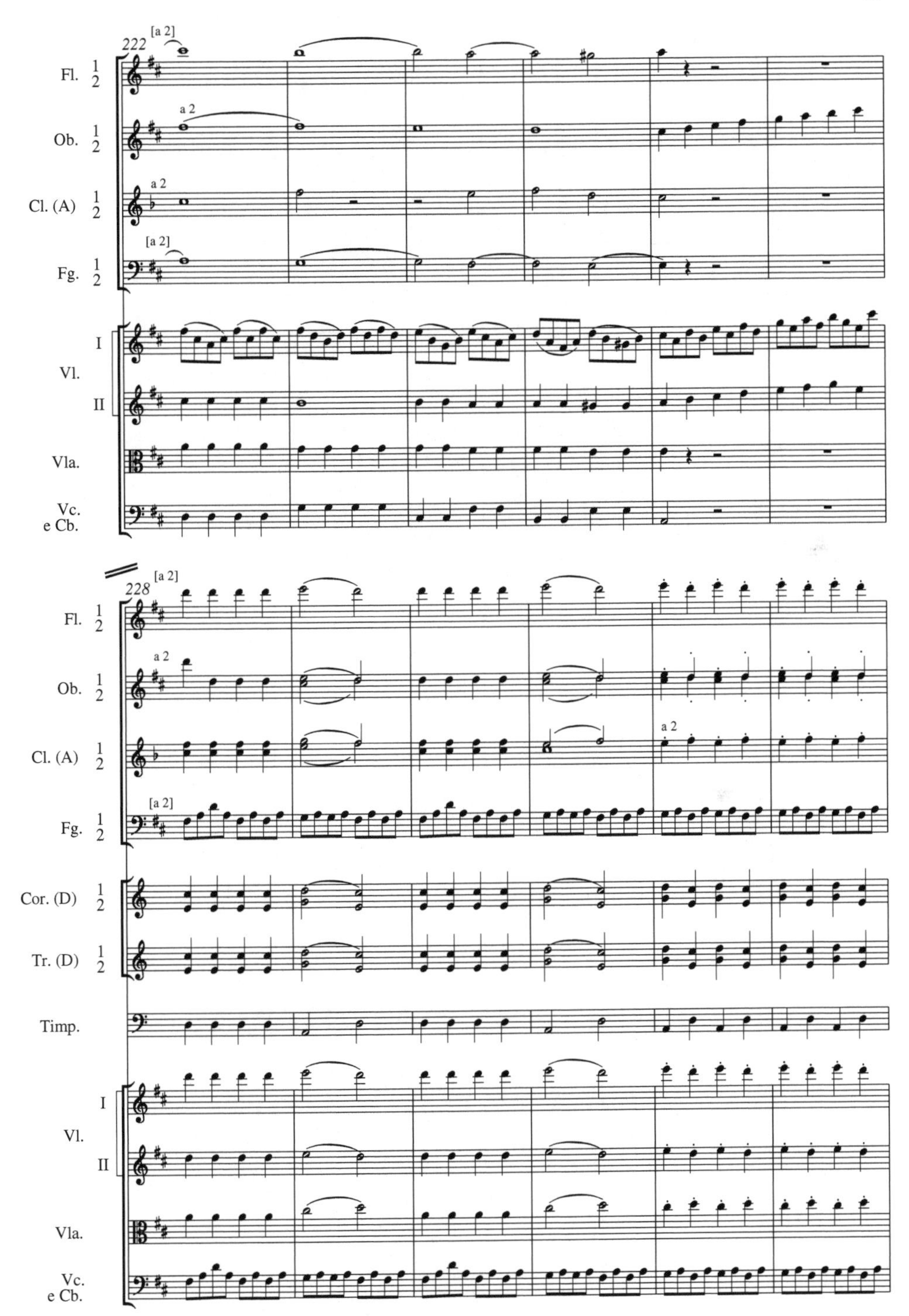
222
[a 2]
Fl. 1 2
a 2
Ob. 1 2
a 2
Cl. (A) 1 2
[a 2]
Fg. 1 2
I
Vl.
II
Vla.
Vc. e Cb.
228
[a 2]
Fl. 1 2
a 2
Ob. 1 2
a 2
Cl. (A) 1 2
[a 2]
Fg. 1 2
Cor. (D) 1 2
Tr. (D) 1 2
Timp.
I
Vl.
II
Vla.
Vc. e Cb.

234
[a 2]
Fl. 1 2
Ob. 1 2
a 2
Cl. (A) 1 2
[a 2]
Fg. 1 2
I
Vl.
II
Vla.
Vc. e Cb.
p

242
Fl. 1 2
[Solo]
Ob. 1 2
Soli
p
I
Vl.
II
pizz.
Vla.
pizz.
Vc. e Cb.

251
[1.]
Fl. 1 2
Solo
Fg. 1 2
[p]
I
Vl.
II
arco
Vla.
arco
Vc. e Cb.
p
257
[a 2]
Fl. 1 2
f
Tutti
Ob. 1 2
f
a 2
Cl. (A) 1 2
f
Tutti
Fg. 1 2
f
Cor. (D) 1 2
f
Tr. (D) 1 2
f
Timp.
f
I
Vl.
II
Vla.
Vc. e Cb.

263
[a 2]
Fl. 1 2
Ob. 1 2
Solo
p
Cl. (A) 1 2
[Soli]
[a 2]
Fg. 1 2
Cor. (D) 1 2
p
Tr. (D) 1 2
Timp.
I
Vl.
II
p
Vla.
p
Vc. e Cb.
270
Fl. 1 2
Solo
p
Ob. 1 2
1.
Cl. (A) 1 2
Fg. 1 2
Solo
p
Cor. (D) 1 2
I
Vl.
II
Vla.
Vc. e Cb.
Vc.
p

277
[a 2]
Fl. 1 2
Tutti
Ob. 1 2
[Tutti]
Cl. (A) 1 2
Tutti
Fg. 1 2
Cor. (D) 1 2
Tr. (D) 1 2
Timp.
I
Vl.
II
Vla.
Vc.
Tutti
Vc. e Cb.
Cb.

282
[a 2]
Fl. 1 2
Ob. 1 2
a 2
Cl. (A) 1 2
a 2
[a 2]
Fg. 1 2
Cor. (D) 1 2
Tr. (D) 1 2
Timp.

I
Vl.
II
Vla.
Vc.
e Cb.

288
[a 2]
Fl. 1 2
Ob. 1 2
a 2
Cl. (A) 1 2
[a 2]
Fg. 1 2
Cor. (D) 1 2
Tr. (D) 1 2
Timp.
I
Vl.
II
Vla.
Vc. e Cb.

II. Andante

Flauto 1 2
Oboe 1 2
Clarinetto (A) 1 2
Fagotto 1 2
Corno (G) 1 2
Tromba (D) 1 2
Violino I II
Viola
Violoncello e Contrabasso
p
fz
7
Vl. I II
Vla.
Vc. e Cb.
Vc.

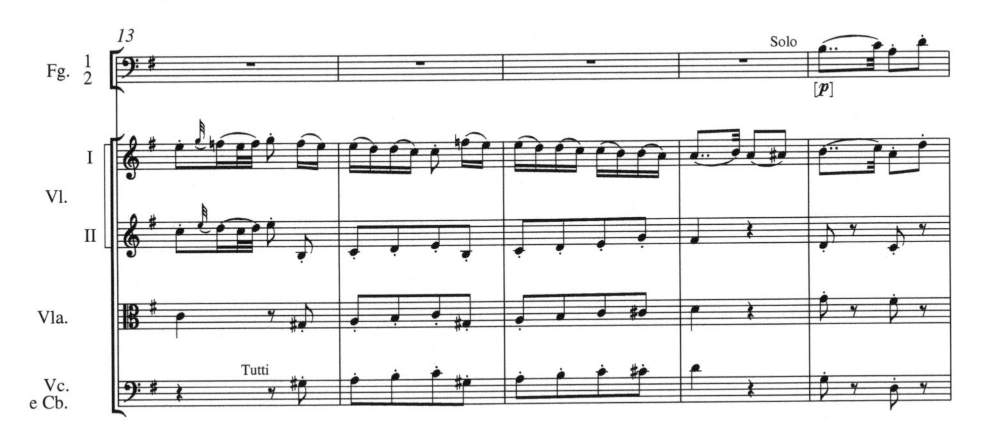
13
Fg. 1 2
Solo
[p]
I
Vl.
II
Vla.
Tutti
Vc. e Cb.

18
1.
Fg. 1 2
fz
p
[Solo]
fz
I
Vl.
II
Vla.
Vc. e Cb.

25
Fg. 1 2
I
Vl.
II
Vla.
Vc. e Cb.

32
Fg. 1 2
Solo
Vl. I II
Vla.
Vc. e Cb.
38
Fl. 1 2
Solo
[a 2]
Ob. 1 2
Tutti
Cl. (A) 1 2
Fg. 1 2
Cor. (G) 1 2
a 2
Tr. (D) 1 2
Timp.
Vl. I II
Vla.
Vc. e Cb.

44
Fl. 1 2
Ob. 1 2
Cl. (A) 1 2
Fg. 1 2
Cor. (G) 1 2
Tr. (D) 1 2
Timp.
Vl. I II
Vla.
Vc. e Cb.
48
[a 2]
a 2

51
[a 2]
Fl. 1 2
a 2
Ob. 1 2
a 2
Fg. 1 2
I
Vl.
II
Vla.
Vc. e Cb.

54
[a 2]
Fl. 1 2
Ob. 1 2
a 2
Fg. 1 2
I
Vl.
II
Vla.
Vc. e Cb.
p
p
p
p

59
Fl. 1 2
[a 2]
f
Ob. 1 2
[fp]
f
[fp]
[fp]
[fp]
Fg. 1 2
[a 2]
f
Cor. (G) 1 2
f
Tr. (D) 1 2
f
Timp.
f
I
Vl.
II
fz
fz
f
fz
[fp]
Vla.
f
Vc.
f
Cb.
f

64
[a 2]
Fl. 1 2
fz
[fp]
Ob. 1 2
Cl. (A) 1 2
[f]
[a 2]
Fg. 1 2
a 2
Cor. (G) 1 2
Tr. (D) 1 2
Timp.
I
Vl.
II
Vla.
Vc. e Cb.

69
[a 2]
Fl. 1 2
Ob. 1 2
Cl. (A) 1 2
[a 2]
Fg. 1 2
Solo
pp
Cor. (G) 1 2
Tr. (D) 1 2
[tr]
Timp.
I
p
Vl.
II
Vla.
Vc.
e Cb.

74
Solo
Fl. 1 2
[p]
fz
p
1.
Fg. 1 2
p
I
Vl.
II
fz
p
Vla.
Vc. e Cb.

79
1.
Fl. 1 2
fz
p
I
Vl.
II
Vla.
Vc. e Cb.

84
1.
[a 2]
Fl. 1 2
p
ff
Ob. 1 2
ff
Cl. (A) 1 2
ff
Solo
[a 2]
Fg. 1 2
[p]
ff
Cor. (G) 1 2
ff
Tr. (D) 1 2
ff
Timp.
ff
I
Vl.
II
p
ff
Vla.
p
ff
Vc. e Cb.
p
ff

88
[a 2]
Fl. 1 2
Ob. 1 2
Cl. (A) 1 2
[a 2]
Fg. 1 2
Cor. (G) 1 2
Tr. (D) 1 2
Timp.
I
Vl.
II
Vla.
Vc. e Cb.
Vc.
p
fz

93
I
Vl.
II
Vla.
Vc. e Cb.
Tutti
p

97
Fl. 1 2
Solo
[p]
fz
p
I
Vl.
II
Vla.
Vc. e Cb.
101
1.
Fl. 1 2
I
Vl.
II
Vla.
Vc. e Cb.

105
I
Vl.
II
Vla.
Vc. e Cb.

108
I
Vl.
II
Vla.
Vc.
e Cb.
crescendo
f

111
Fl. 1 2
Ob. 1 2
Fg. 1 2
Solo
p
più largo
I
Vl.
II
Vla.
Vc.
e Cb.

116
1.
Fl. 1 2
1°tempo
più largo
1°tempo
Ob. 1 2
Fg. 1 2
[p]
Timp.
pp
Vl. I
Vl. II
Vla.
Vc. e Cb.
122
Tutti
ff
fz
Solo
f
Cor. (G) 1 2
Timp.

126
[a 2]
Fl. 1 2
Ob. 1 2
Fg. 1 2
1.
Cor. (G) 1 2
a 2
I
Vl.
II
Vla.
Vc. e Cb.
129
[a 2]
Solo
a 2

133
1.
[cresc.]
Fl. 1 2
Ob. 1 2
[1.]
[a 2]
Fg. 1 2
Cor. (G) 1 2
[a 2]
Tr. (D) 1 2
Timp.
I
Vl.
II
Vla.
Vc. e Cb.
138
Tutti
Fl. 1 2
Solo
Fg. 1 2
I
Vl.
II
Vla.
Vc. e Cb.

142
[a 2]
Fl. 1 2
Ob. 1 2
Solo
p
Fg. 1 2
1.
Cor. (G) 1 2
p
I
Vl.
II
Vla.
Vc.
e Cb.
147
[a 2]
Fl. 1 2
pp
Ob. 1 2
1.
pp
Fg. 1 2
1.
[a 2]
pp
Cor. (G) 1 2
Soli
pp
I
Vl.
pp
II
pp
Vla.
pp
Vc.
e Cb.
pp

III. Menuet

Allegro

5
[a 2]
Fl. 1 2
fz
fz
tr
p
Ob. 1 2
tr
1.
fz
p
fz
Cl. (A) 1 2
tr
tr
[a 2]
Fg. 1 2
fz
a 2
Cor. (D) 1 2
tr
p
Tr. (D) 1 2
tr
Timp.
I
Vl.
II
tr
fz
p
tr
fz
p
Vla.
tr
fz
p
Vc. e Cb.
fz
p
11
[a 2]
Fl. 1 2
fz
tr
1.
Ob. 1 2
tr
1 2
a 2
tr
I
Vl.
II
fz
tr
tr
[fp]
Vla.
fz
tr
Vc. e Cb.
[fp]

Fl. 1 2
Ob. 1 2
Cl. (A) 1 2
Fg. 1 2
Cor. (D) 1 2
Tr. (D) 1 2
Timp.
Vl. I II
Vla.
Vc. e Cb.
[a 2]
17
a 2
2.
1.
[f]
Vc.
Tutti

23
[a 2]
Fl. 1 2
Ob. 1 2
Cl. (A) 1 2
[a 2]
[Solo]
Fg. 1 2
p
Cor. (D) 1 2
p
a 2
Tr. (D) 1 2
I
Vl.
II
p
p
Vla.
p
Vc. e Cb.
p
29
[Solo]
[a 2]
Fl. 1 2
fz
fz
f
1.
Ob. 1 2
fz
fz
f
[1.]
Fg. 1 2
[p]
1 2
Timp.
pp
cresc.
I
Vl.
f
II
f
Vla.
f
Vc. e Cb.

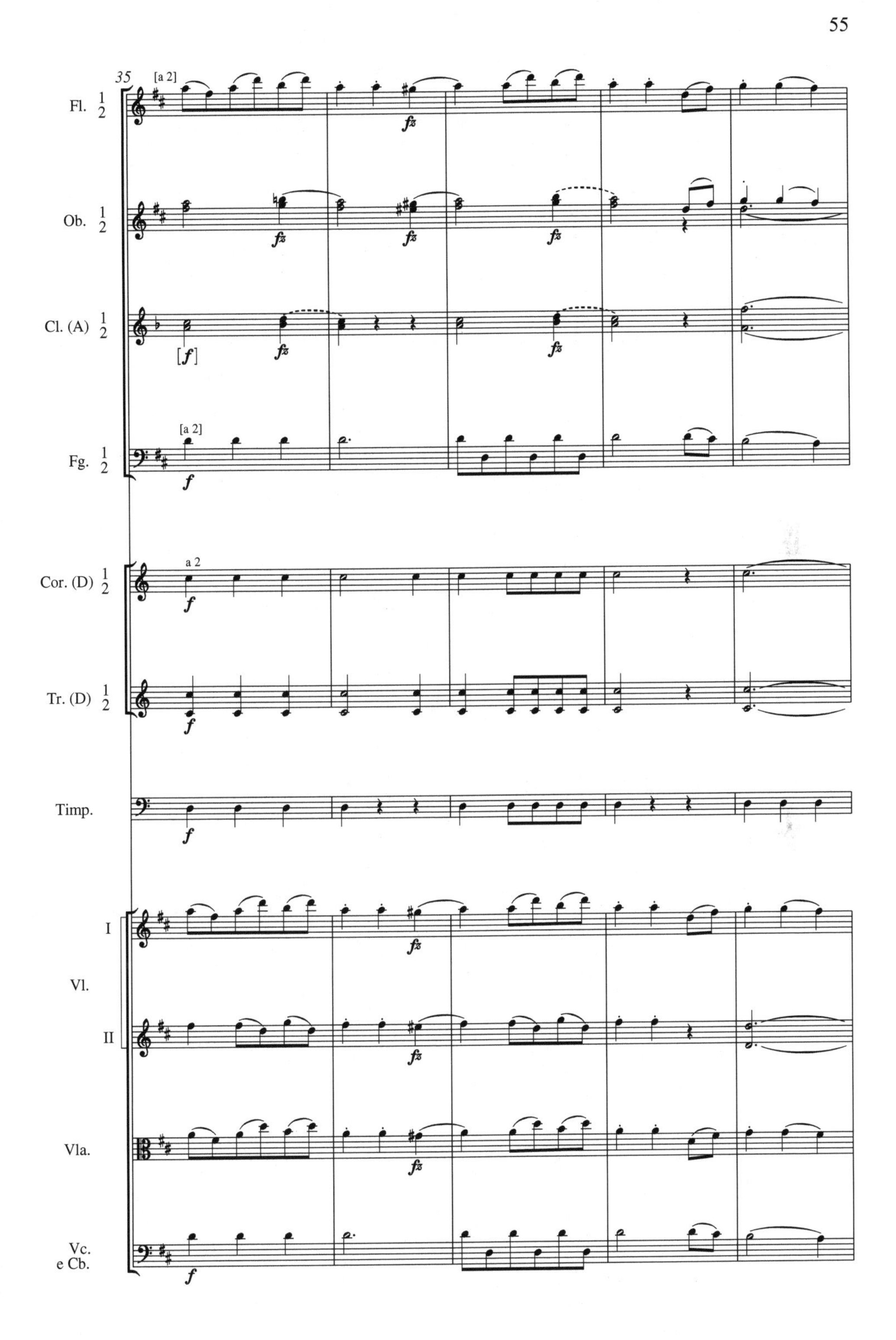
35
[a 2]
Fl. 1 2
fz
Ob. 1 2
fz
fz
fz
Cl. (A) 1 2
[f]
fz
fz
[a 2]
Fg. 1 2
f
a 2
Cor. (D) 1 2
f
Tr. (D) 1 2
f
Timp.
f
I
Vl.
II
fz
fz
Vla.
fz
Vc. e Cb.
f

40
[a 2]
Fl. 1 2
fz
tr
Ob. 1 2
a 2
Cl. (A) 1 2
Fg. 1 2
Cor. (D) 1 2
a 2
Tr. (D) 1 2
Timp.
I
Vl.
II
[fp]
Vla.
Vc. e Cb.

47
[a 2]
Fl. 1 2
p
f
Ob. 1 2
p
f
a 2
Cl. (A) 1 2
[f]
[a 2]
Fg. 1 2
p
f
Cor. (D) 1 2
f
Tr. (D) 1 2
f
Timp.
f
I
Vl.
II
p
f
Vla.
p
f
Vc. e Cb.
p
f
Trio
Solo
53
Ob. 1 2
p
Fg. 1 2
Solo
[p]
I
Vl.
II
p
pizz.
[p]
Vla.
pizz.
[p]
Vc. e Cb.
pizz.
[p]

59
1.
Fg. 1 2
I
Vl.
II
Vla.
Vc. e Cb.
65
[Solo]
Fl. 1 2
[p]
2. Solo
1.[Solo]
Ob. 1 2
[p]
1.
Solo
Fg. 1 2
I
Vl.
arco
II
Vla.
Vc. e Cb.
71
1.
Fl. 1 2
1.
2.
Ob. 1 2
1.
Fg. 1 2
I
Vl.
II
arco
Vla.
arco
Vc. e Cb.

77
Ob. 1 2
Fg. 1 2
1.
I
Vl.
II
pizz.
Vla.
Vc. e Cb.

84
[Solo]
Fl. 1 2
Ob. 1 2
1.
Fg. 1 2
I
Vl.
II
arco
Vla.
Vc. e Cb.

Menuet da capo

IV. Finale

Spiritoso
Flauto 1 2
Oboe 1 2
Clarinetto (A) 1 2
Fagotto 1 2
Corno (D) 1 2
Tromba (D) 1 2
Timpani
Violino I
Violino II
Viola
Vc.
Violoncello e Contrabasso
p
7
Ob. 1 2
Fg. 1 2
Cor. (D) 1 2
Vl. I
Vl. II
Vla.
Vc. e Cb.
1.
[p]
[a 2]
Cb.

14
Fl. 1 2
[a 2]
f
Ob. 1 2
1.
f
Cl. (A) 1 2
f
Fg. 1 2
[a 2]
f
Cor. (D) 1 2
f
Tr. (D) 1 2
f
Timp.
f
Vl.
I
f
II
f
Vla.
f
Vc. e Cb.
Tutti
f

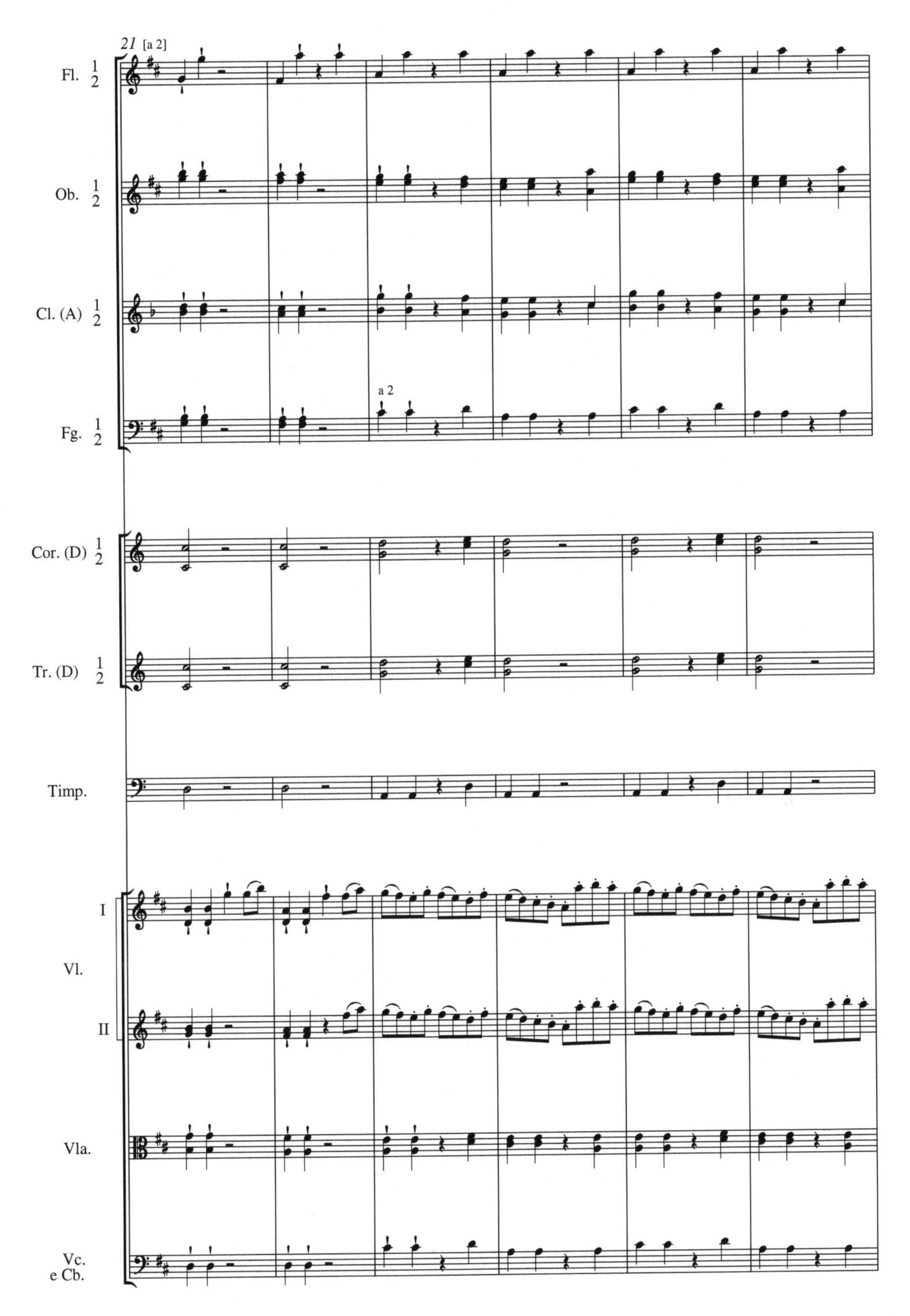
21
[a 2]
Fl. 1 2
Ob. 1 2
Cl. (A) 1 2
a 2
Fg. 1 2
Cor. (D) 1 2
Tr. (D) 1 2
Timp.
I
Vl.
II
Vla.
Vc. e Cb.

27
[a 2]
Fl. 1 2
Ob. 1 2
a 2
Cl. (A) 1 2
[a 2]
Fg. 1 2
ff
fz
Cor. (D) 1 2
Tr. (D) 1 2
Timp.
I
Vl.
II
Vla.
Vc. e Cb.
[ff]

33
[a 2]
Fl. 1 2
Ob. 1 2
Cl. (A) 1 2
Fg. 1 2
Cor. (D) 1 2
Tr. (D) 1 2
Timp.
Vl. I II
Vla.
Vc. e Cb.

40
[a 2]
Fl. 1 2
fz
Ob. 1 2
a 2
Cl. (A) 1 2
Fg. 1 2
Cor. (D) 1 2
Tr. (D) 1 2
Timp.
I
Vl.
II
Vla.
Vc. e Cb.

47
[a 2]
Fl. 1 2
Ob. 1 2
a 2
Cl. (A) 1 2
Fg. 1 2
Cor. (D) 1 2
Vl. I II
Vla.
Vc. e Cb.
54
Tr. (D) 1 2
Timp.

60
[a 2]
Fl. 1 2
fz
Ob. 1 2
Cl. (A) 1 2
Fg. 1 2
Cor. (D) 1 2
Tr. (D) 1 2
Timp.
Vl. I II
Vla.
Vc. e Cb.
p
66
Solo
Vc.
Cb.

73
[a 2]
Fl. 1 2
f
Ob. 1 2
f
Cl. (A) 1 2
f
Tutti
Fg. 1 2
f
a 2
Cor. (D) 1 2
f
a 2
Tr. (D) 1 2
f
Timp.
I
Vl.
II
f
f
Vla.
f
Vc.
f
Cb.
f

78
[a 2]
Fl. 1 2
Ob. 1 2
Cl. (A) 1 2
Fg. 1 2
Cor. (D) 1 2
a 2
Tr. (D) 1 2
Timp.
I
Vl.
II
Vla.
Vc.
Cb.

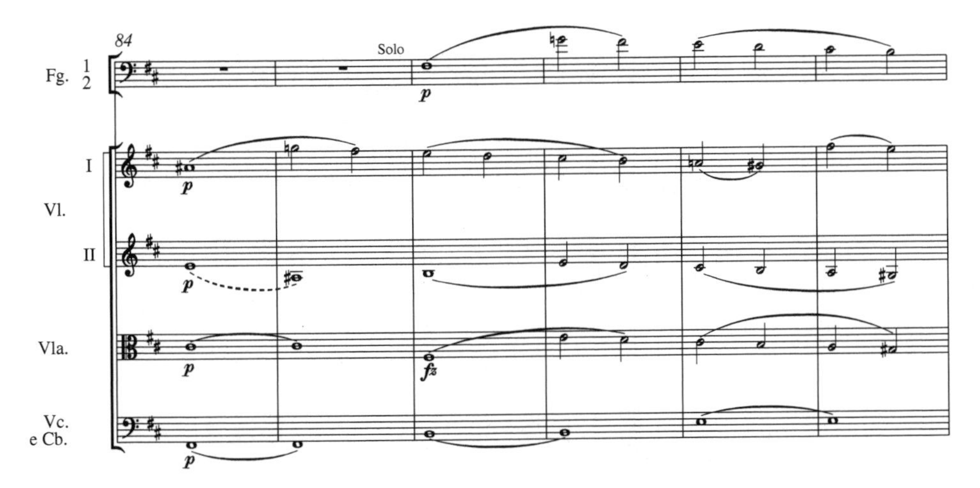
84
Solo
Fg. 1 2
Vl. I
II
Vla.
Vc. e Cb.

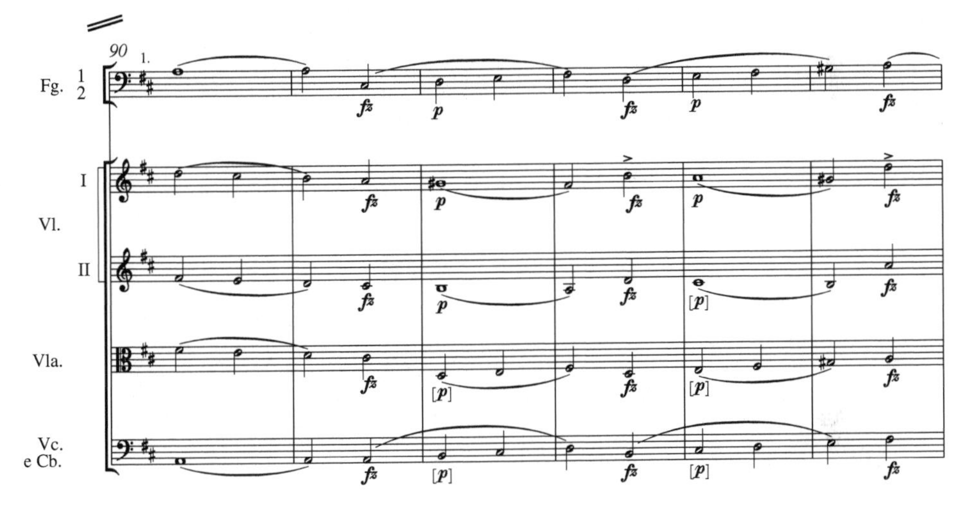
90
1.
Fg. 1 2
Vl. I
II
Vla.
Vc. e Cb.

96
1.
Fg. 1 2
Vl. I
II
Vla.
Vc. e Cb.

102
[a 2]
Fl. 1 2
Ob. 1 2
Cl. (A) 1 2
Fg. 1 2
Cor. (D) 1 2
Tr. (D) 1 2
Timp.
I
Vl.
II
Vla.
Vc.
Cb.

108
[a 2]
Fl. 1 2
Ob. 1 2
Cl. (A) 1 2
Fg. 1 2
a 2
Cor. (D) 1 2
a 2
Tr. (D) 1 2
Timp.
I
Vl.
II
Vla.
Vc.
Cb.

114
[a 2]
Fl. 1 2
fz
p
1
Ob. 1 2
Cl. (A) 1 2
a 2
Fg. 1 2
a 2
Cor. (D) 1 2
Tr. (D) 1 2
Timp.
I
Vl.
II
Vla.
Vc.
Cb.

118
2
[a 2]
Fl. 1 2
Ob. 1 2
Cl. (A) 1 2
Fg. 1 2
[a 2]
Cor. (D) 1 2
Tr. (D) 1 2
Timp.
I
Vl.
II
Vla.
Vc. e Cb.

125
[a 2]
Fl. 1 2
Ob. 1 2
a 2
Cl. (A) 1 2
[a 2]
Fg. 1 2
fz
Cor. (D) 1 2
Tr. (D) 1 2
Timp.
I
Vl.
II
Vla.
Vc. e Cb.
fz

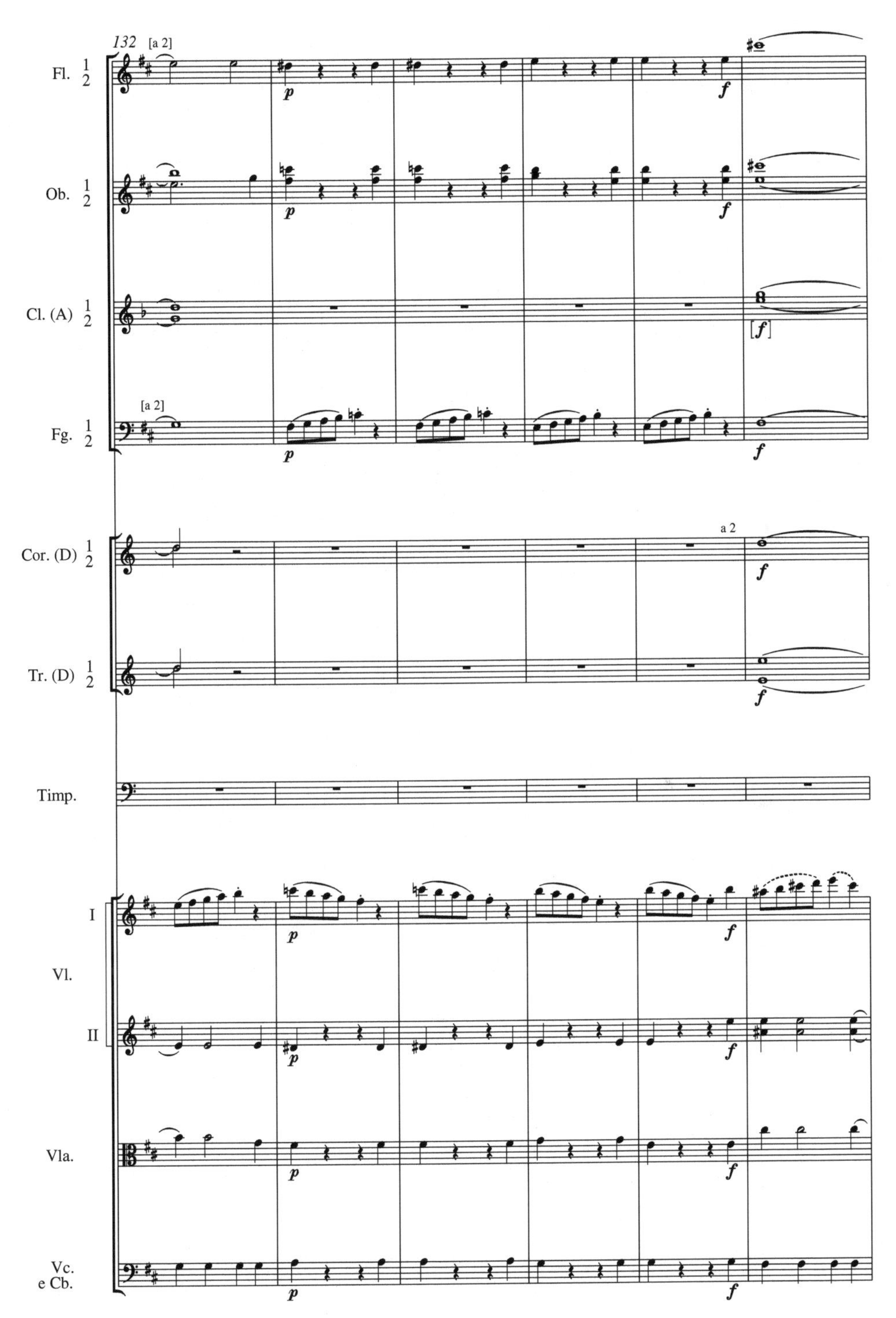
132
[a 2]
Fl. 1 2
Ob. 1 2
Cl. (A) 1 2
[a 2]
Fg. 1 2
a 2
Cor. (D) 1 2
Tr. (D) 1 2
Timp.
I
Vl.
II
Vla.
Vc. e Cb.

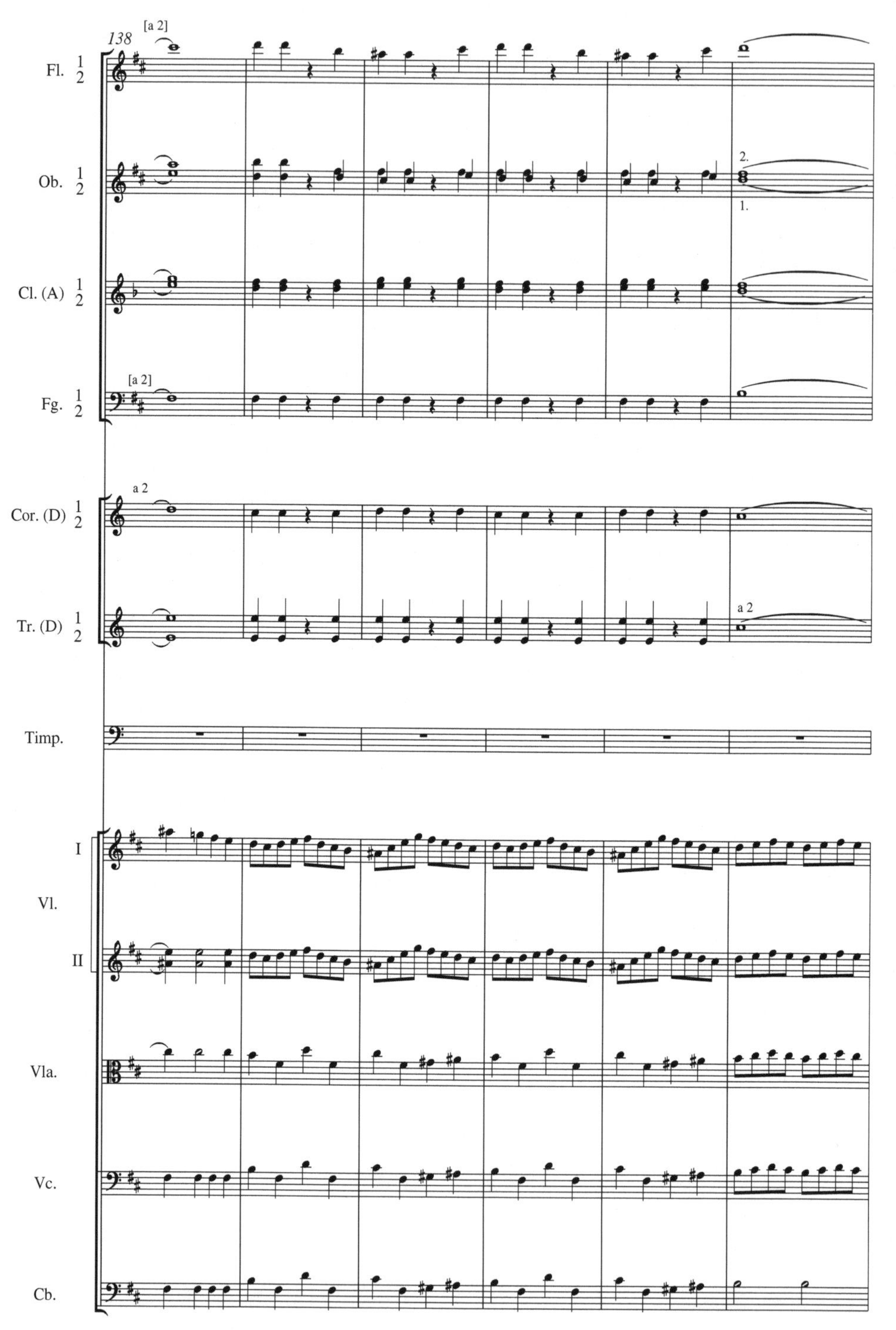
138
[a 2]
Fl. 1 2
Ob. 1 2
2.
1.
Cl. (A) 1 2
[a 2]
Fg. 1 2
a 2
Cor. (D) 1 2
Tr. (D) 1 2
a 2
Timp.
I
Vl.
II
Vla.
Vc.
Cb.

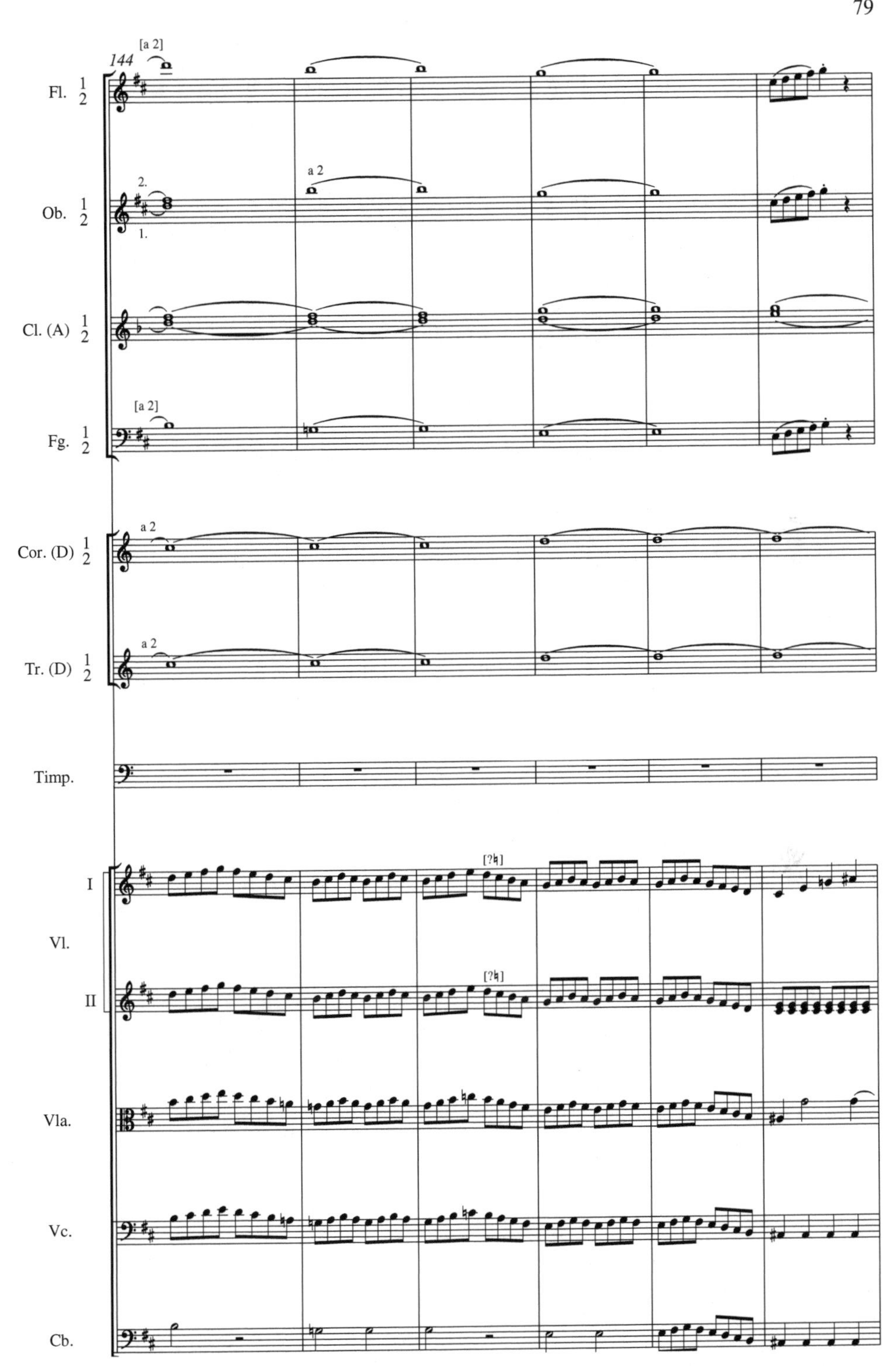
144
[a 2]
Fl. 1 2
a 2
2.
Ob. 1 2
1.
Cl. (A) 1 2
[a 2]
Fg. 1 2
a 2
Cor. (D) 1 2
a 2
Tr. (D) 1 2
Timp.
[?♮]
I
Vl.
[?♮]
II
Vla.
Vc.
Cb.

150
[a 2]
Fl. 1 2
a 2
Ob. 1 2
Cl. (A) 1 2
a 2
[a 2]
Fg. 1 2
a 2
Cor. (D) 1 2
a 2
Tr. (D) 1 2
Timp.
I
Vl.
II
Vla.
Vc.
e Cb.

156
[a 2]
Fl. 1 2
Ob. 1 2
a 2
Cl. (A) 1 2
Fg. 1 2
[a 2]
Cor. (D) 1 2
Tr. (D) 1 2
Timp.
I
Vl.
II
Vla.
Vc. e Cb.

163
[a 2]
Fl. 1 2
[Solo]
p
Ob. 1 2
1. [Solo]
p
Cl. (A) 1 2
Fg. 1 2
[a 2]
Solo
p
Cor. (D) 1 2
Tr. (D) 1 2
I
Vl.
II
p
Vla.
p
Vc.
p
Cb.
p
170
[1.]
Fl. 1 2
1.
Ob. 1 2
1.
Fg. 1 2
I
Vl.
II
p
Vla.
Vc.
Cb.

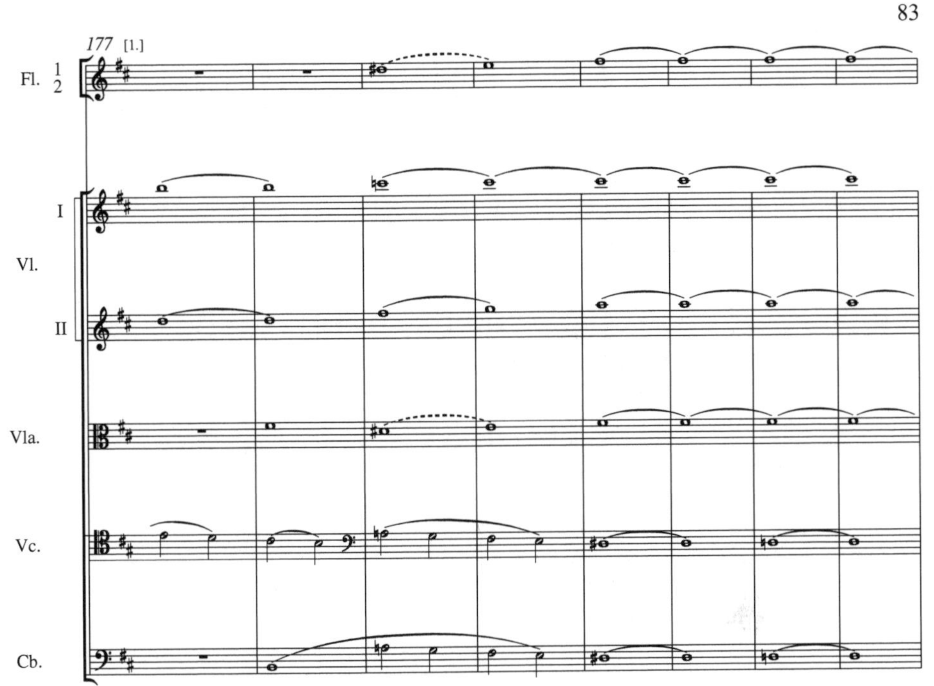
177
[1.]
Fl. 1 2
I
Vl.
II
Vla.
Vc.
Cb.

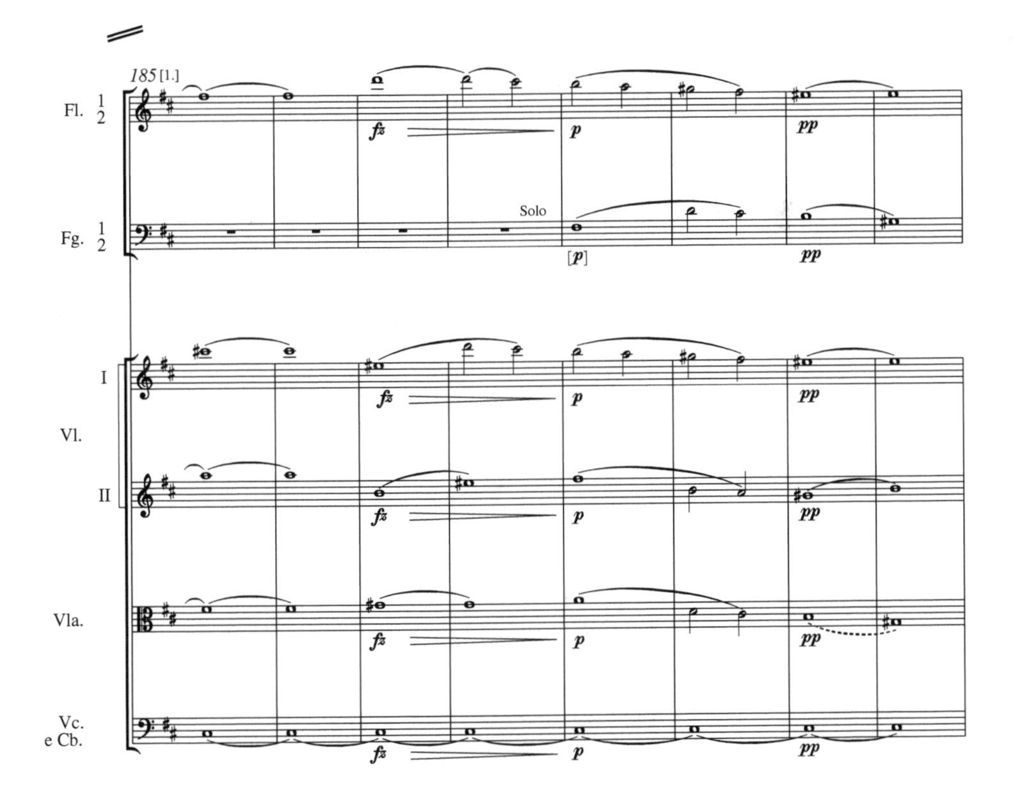
185
[1.]
Fl. 1 2
fz
p
pp
Solo
Fg. 1 2
[p]
pp
I
Vl.
II
Vla.
Vc. e Cb.

193
[1.]
[a 2]
Fl.
1
2
p
[Tutti]
Ob.
1
2
p
Cl. (A)
1
2
1.
[Tutti]
Fg.
1
2
p
Cor. (D)
1
2
p
Tr. (D)
1
2
Timp.
I
Vl.
II
[p]
[p]
Vla.
[p]
Vc.
p
Cb.

200
[a 2]
Fl. 1 2
Ob. 1 2
Cl. (A) 1 2
[a 2]
Fg. 1 2
Cor. (D) 1 2
Tr. (D) 1 2
Timp.
I
Vl.
II
Vla.
Vc.
Cb.
f

207 [a 2]
Fl. 1 2
Ob. 1 2
Cl. (A) 1 2
[a 2]
Fg. 1 2
Cor. (D) 1 2
f
a 2
Tr. (D) 1 2
a 2
Timp.
I
Vl.
II
Vla.
Vc. e Cb.

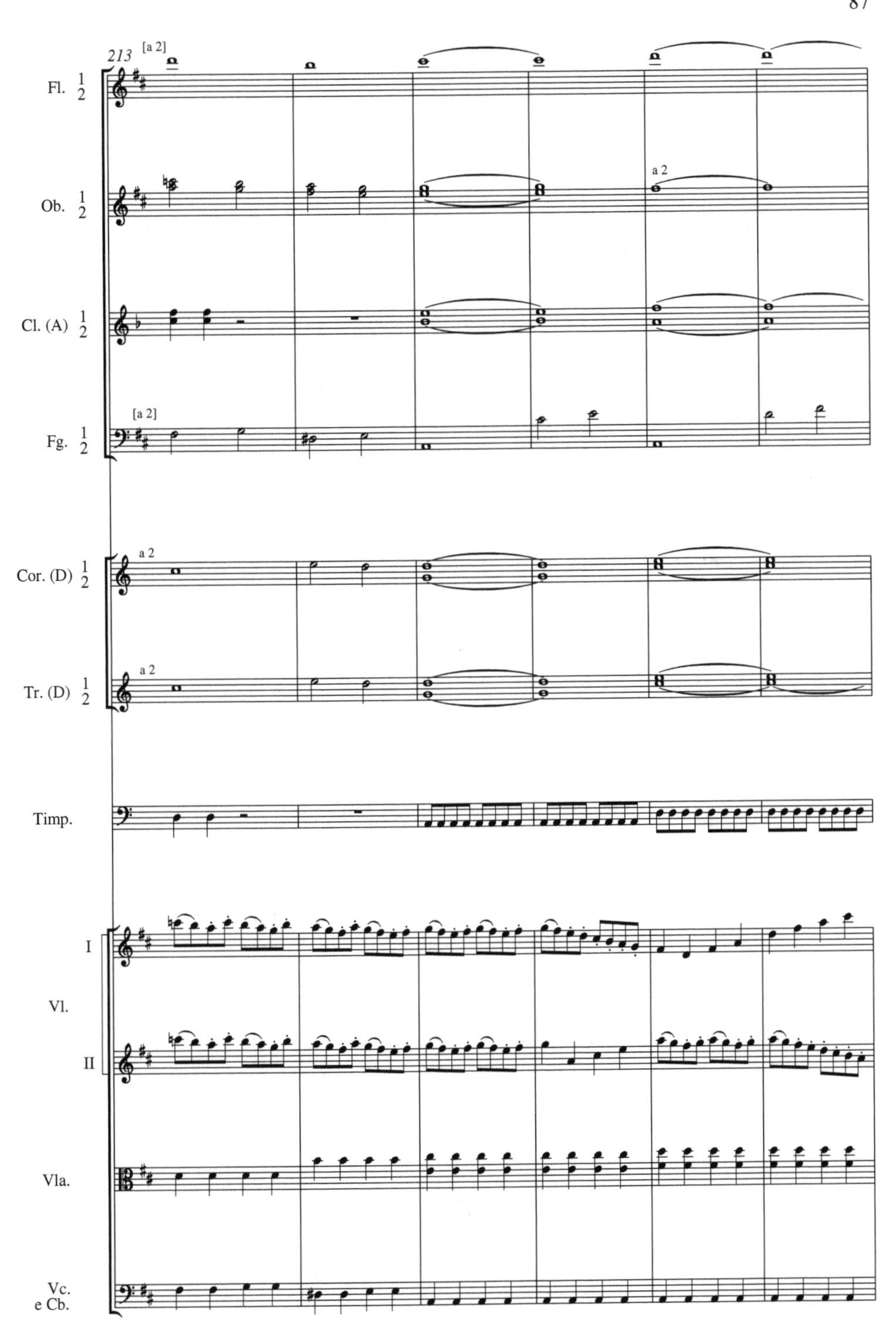
213
[a 2]
Fl. 1 2
Ob. 1 2
a 2
Cl. (A) 1 2
[a 2]
Fg. 1 2
a 2
Cor. (D) 1 2
a 2
Tr. (D) 1 2
Timp.
I
Vl.
II
Vla.
Vc.
e Cb.

219
[a 2]
Fl. 1 2
fz
2.
1.
Ob. 1 2
1.
2.
Cl. (A) 1 2
a 2
[a 2]
Fg. 1 2
Cor. (D) 1 2
Tr. (D) 1 2
Timp.
I
Vl.
II
Vla.
Vc. e Cb.

225
[a 2]
Fl. 1 2
Ob. 1 2
a 2
Cl. (A) 1 2
[a 2]
Fg. 1 2
fz
fz
Cor. (D) 1 2
a 2
fz
fz
Tr. (D) 1 2
Timp.
I
Vl.
II
Vla.
fz
fz
Vc. e Cb.
fz
fz

232
[a 2]
Fl. 1 2
fz
a 2
Ob. 1 2
Cl. (A) 1 2
[a 2]
Fg. 1 2
Cor. (D) 1 2
Tr. (D) 1 2
Timp.
[fp]
I
Vl.
II
Vla.
Vc. e Cb.

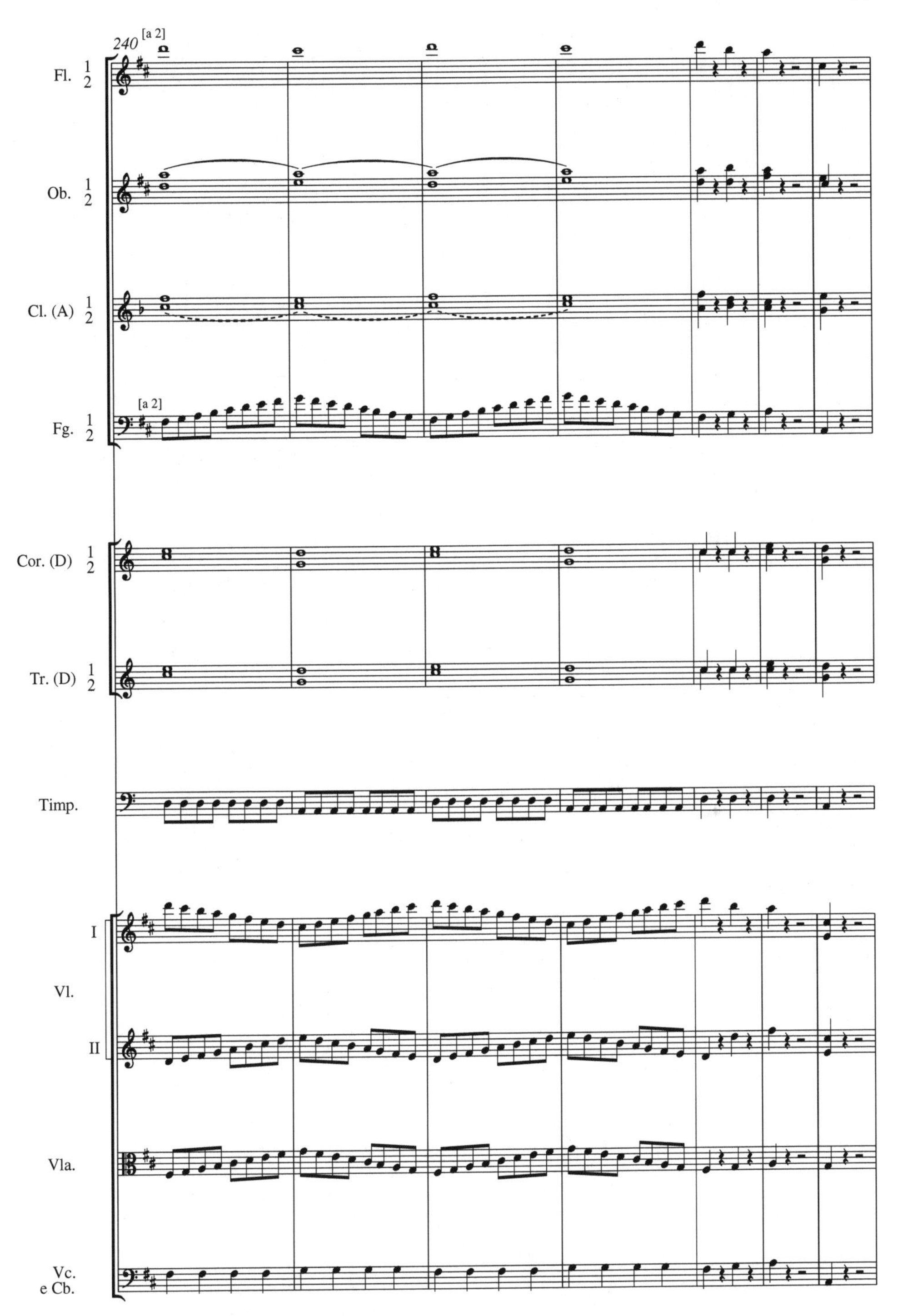
240
[a 2]
Fl. 1 2
Ob. 1 2
Cl. (A) 1 2
[a 2]
Fg. 1 2
Cor. (D) 1 2
Tr. (D) 1 2
Timp.
I
Vl.
II
Vla.
Vc.
e Cb.

247
Solo
Fl. 1 2
p
I
Vl.
II
Vla.
Vc. e Cb.
fz

255
1.
Fl. 1 2
fz
[fp]
p
I
Vl.
II
Vla.
Vc. e Cb.
pp

263
1.
[a 2]
Fl. 1 2
Ob. 1 2
Cl. (A) 1 2
[a 2]
Fg. 1 2
Cor. (D) 1 2
Tr. (D) 1 2
Timp.
I
Vl.
II
Vla.
Vc. e Cb.

270
[a 2]
Fl. 1 2
fz
fz
Ob. 1 2
fz
[fz]
fz
fz
Solo
Cl. (A) 1 2
[a 2]
Fg. 1 2
Cor. (D) 1 2
a 2
Tr. (D) 1 2
a 2
Timp.
I
Vl.
II
fz
fz
fz
fz
Vla.
Vc.
e Cb.

276
Solo
Fl. 1 2
Ob. 1 2
Vl. I II
Vla.
Vc. e Cb.
283
1.
[a 2]
Tutti
a 2
Cl. (A) 1 2
Fg. 1 2
Cor. (D) 1 2
Tr. (D) 1 2
Timp.
Vc.
Cb.

290
Fl. 1 2
[a 2]
Fg. 1 2
[a 2]
fz
Vl. I II
Vla.
Vc.
Cb.
295 [a 2]
Fl. 1 2
[a 2]
Fg. 1 2
Vl. I II
Vla.
Vc.
Cb.

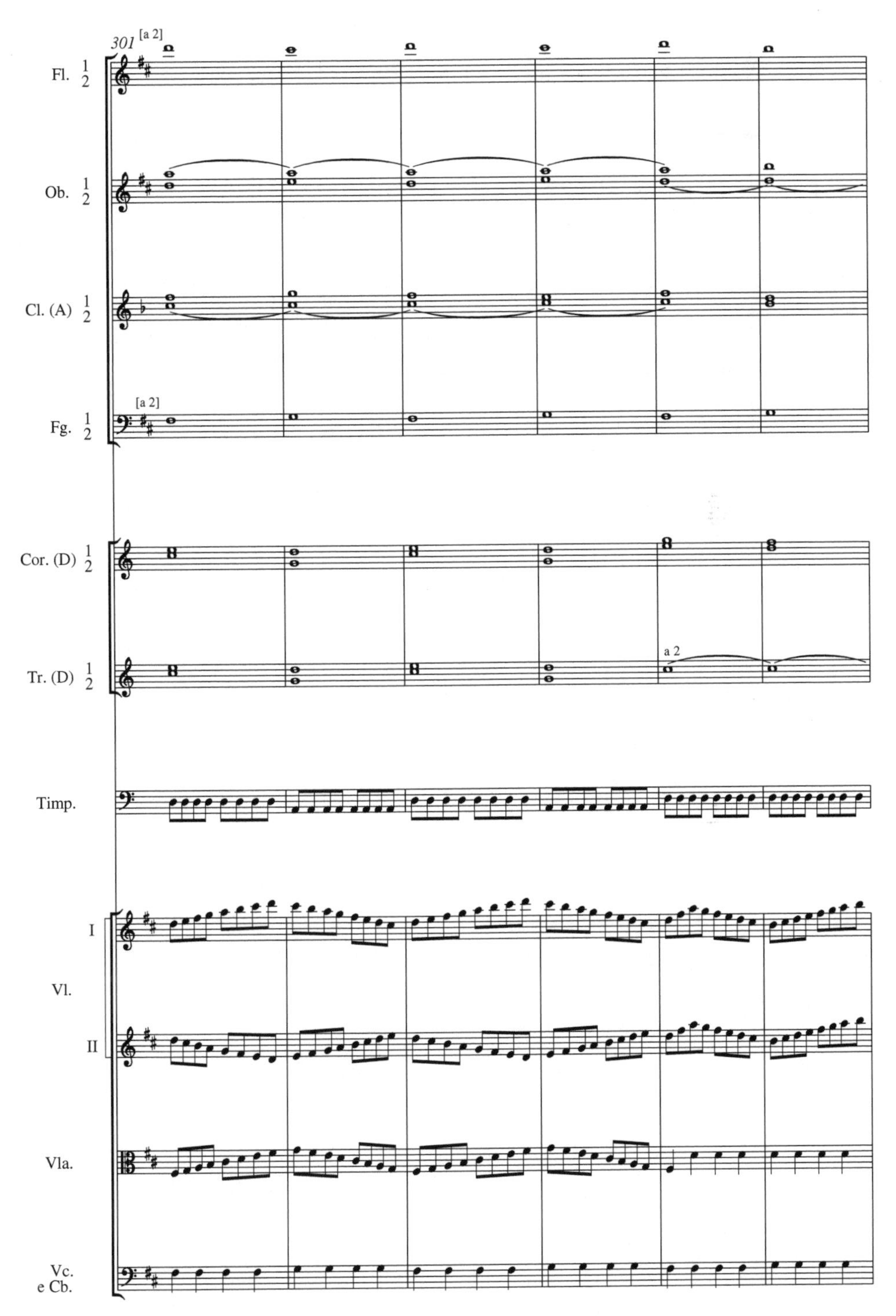
301
[a 2]
Fl. 1 2
Ob. 1 2
Cl. (A) 1 2
[a 2]
Fg. 1 2
Cor. (D) 1 2
a 2
Tr. (D) 1 2
Timp.
I
Vl.
II
Vla.
Vc.
e Cb.

307
[a 2]
Fl. 1 2
Ob. 1 2
Cl. (A) 1 2
Fg. 1 2
Cor. (D) 1 2
Tr. (D) 1 2
Timp.
Vl. I II
Vla.
Vc.
Cb.
a 2
ff
f
[ff]
[f]
1.
2.

314
[a 2]
Fl. 1 2
fz
Ob. 1 2
a 2
Cl. (A) 1 2
Fg. 1 2
[a 2]
Cor. (D) 1 2
Tr. (D) 1 2
Timp.
I
Vl.
II
Vla.
Vc.
Cb.

321
[a 2]
Fl. 1 2
a 2
Ob. 1 2
a 2
Cl. (A) 1 2
[a 2]
Fg. 1 2
Cor. (D) 1 2
Tr. (D) 1 2
Timp.
I
Vl.
II
Vla.
Vc. e Cb.
p
fz
f
[fp]

Fine Laus Deo

APPENDIX/ANHANG

Mov. II, b.106ff., original version/2. Satz, T. 106ff., Urfassung

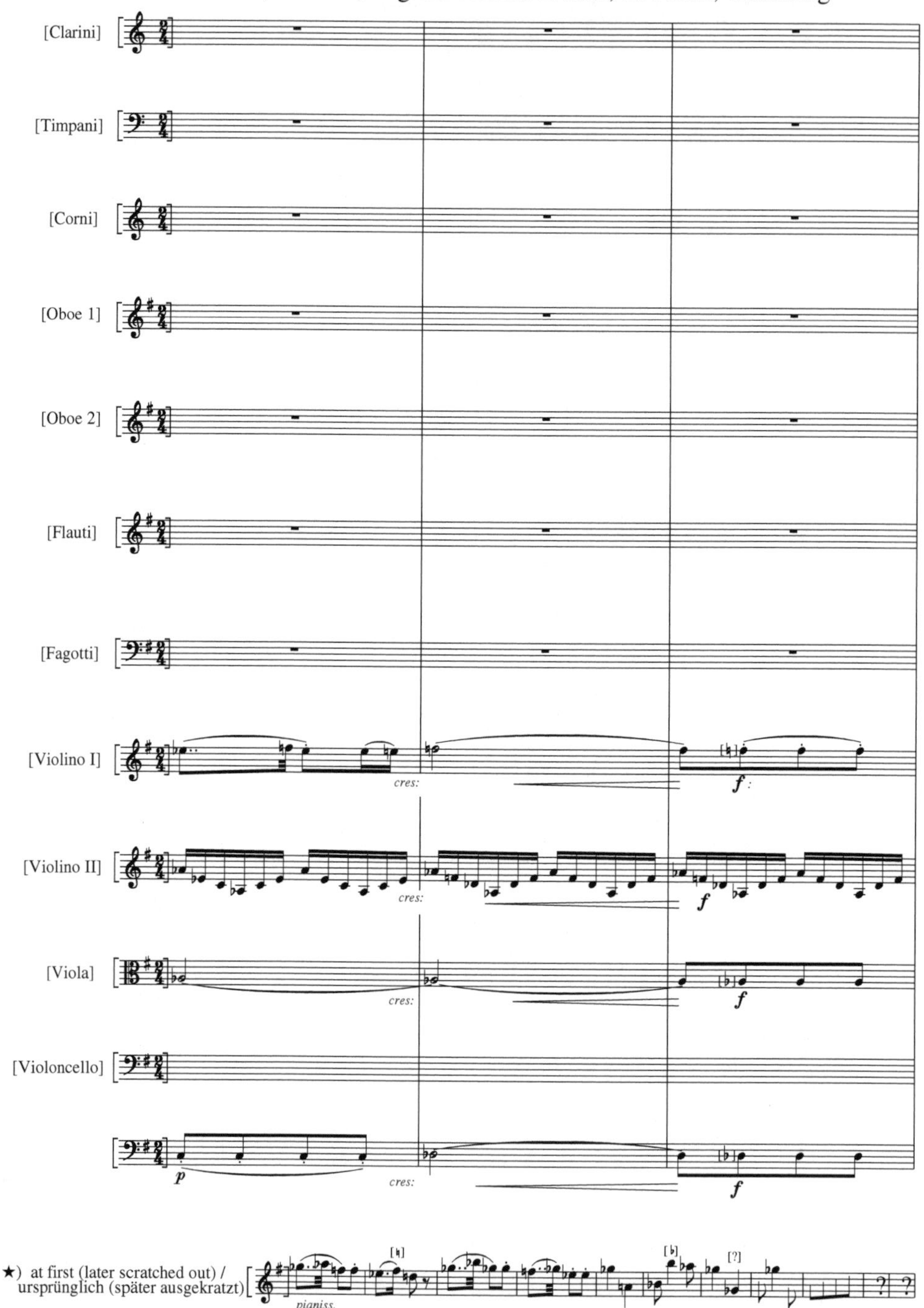

★) at first (later scratched out) / ursprünglich (später ausgekratzt)

[Clarini]
[Timpani]
[Corni]
[Oboe 1]
[Solo]
p
[Oboe 2]
[Solo]
p
[Flauti]
[Solo]
p
[Fagotti]
Solo
p
più largo
1mo tempo
[Violino I]
★)
p
[Violino II]
p
[Viola]
p
[Violoncello]
NB
p